THE 1912 AND 1915 GUSTAV STICKLEY CRAFTSMAN FURNITURE CATALOGS

Gustav Stickley

A Joint Publication of
THE ATHENAEUM OF PHILADELPHIA
AND
DOVER PUBLICATIONS, INC., NEW YORK

Published in Canada by General Publishing Company, Ltd., 30 Lesmill Road, Don Mills, Toronto, Ontario.

Published in the United Kingdom by Constable and Company, Ltd., 3 The Lanchesters, 162–164 Fulham Palace Road, London W6 9ER.

This Athenaeum of Philadelphia/Dover edition, first published in 1991, is a republication of the 1912 catalog of The Craftsman Workshops, Eastwood, N.Y., and the 1915(?) catalog of The Craftsman Department of Interior Furnishings, New York. A preface and a publisher's note have been added. We are grateful to Victor M. Linoff for the loan of the 1912 catalog for reproduction.

Manufactured in the United States of America
Dover Publications, Inc., 31 East 2nd Street, Mineola, N.Y. 11501

Library of Congress Cataloging-in-Publication Data

Stickley, Gustav, 1858–1942.
    [Catalogue of craftsman furniture]
    The 1912 and 1915 Gustav Stickley craftsman furniture catalogs / Gustav Stickley.
       p.   cm.
    Reprint (1st work). Originally published: 1912.
    Reprint (2nd work). Originally published: 1915.
    Includes bibliographical references.
    ISBN 0-486-26676-1 (pbk.)
    1. Stickley, Gustav, 1858–1942—Catalogs. 2. Furniture—United States—History—20th century—Catalogs. I. Title.
NK2439.S8A4 1991
749.213—dc20
                                           91-9877
                                              CIP

PREFACE TO THE ATHENAEUM/DOVER EDITION

THIS REPRINT EDITION of two Craftsman Furniture catalogs is one in a series of reprints of books and trade catalogs published by special agreement between The Athenaeum of Philadelphia and Dover Publications, Inc. The objective of this series is to make available to the greatest possible audience rare and often fragile documents from the extensive collections of The Athenaeum in sturdy and inexpensive editions.

The Athenaeum of Philadelphia is an independent research library with museum collections founded in 1814 to collect materials "connected with the history and antiquities of America, and the useful arts, and generally to disseminate useful knowledge." It is housed in a handsomely restored National Historic Landmark building near Independence Hall in the heart of the historic area of Philadelphia.

As the collections expanded over the past 175 years, The Athenaeum refined its objectives. Today the library concentrates on nineteenth- and early twentieth-century social and cultural history, particularly architecture and interior design where the collections are nationally significant. The library is freely open to serious investigators, and it annually attracts thousands of readers: graduate students and senior scholars, architects, interior designers, museum curators and private owners of historic houses.

In addition to 130,000 architectural drawings, 25,000 historic photographs and several million manuscripts, The Athenaeum's library is particularly rich in original works on architecture, interior design and domestic technology. In the latter area the publications of manufacturers and dealers in architectural elements and interior embellishments have been found to be particularly useful to design professionals and historic house owners who are concerned with the restoration or the recreation of period interiors. Consequently, many of the reprints in this series are drawn from this collection. The Athenaeum's holdings are particularly strong in areas such as paint colors, lighting fixtures, wallpaper, heating and kitchen equipment, plumbing and household furniture.

The modern Athenaeum also sponsors a diverse program of lectures, chamber music concerts and exhibitions. It publishes books that reflect the institution's collecting interests, and it administers several trusts that provide awards and research grants to recognize literary achievement and to encourage outstanding scholarship in architectural history throughout the United States. For further information, write The Athenaeum of Philadelphia, East Washington Square, Philadelphia, PA 19106-3794.

ROGER W. MOSS
Executive Director

PUBLISHER'S NOTE

THE PROGRESSIVE MOVEMENT that surged up in the wake of the excesses of the Gilded Age and the disruptions of America's sweeping industrialization found its expression not only politically—most notably in the major reforms of Theodore Roosevelt's administration—but also in such aesthetic manifestations as houses and interior furnishings. The style popularly (if carelessly) known by such diverse names as Craftsman, Mission and Arts & Crafts was, in the context of its times, revolutionary. From the welter of ornamented historical styles that the later nineteenth century favored— Renaissance Italianate, English baronial, French rococo and the rest—its emergence came as a bracing shock.

Gustav Stickley (1858–1942) was the most influential American exponent of the new design style and ethic. He and his brothers had founded their first furniture company in 1884; in 1899, after many further ventures, he took over as sole head of his own company in Eastwood, N.Y. He returned from his first trip to England and Europe, around 1898, filled with the vision of William Morris and John Ruskin, the great English heralds of a new social and aesthetic order, and commenced to produce designs strongly akin to those of the English Arts & Crafts movement. From 1901 to 1916 his journal, *The Craftsman*, brought an entire worldview to its readers through essays on art and society, fiction, poetry and art reproductions, in addition to its many photographs and plans of houses and furniture.

Stickley caught and helped shape the spirit and taste of the era. By 1912, the date of the earlier catalog reprinted here, Stickley's Craftsman furniture and houses were the most imitated in the country. The circulation of *The Craftsman* had doubled in the previous year alone, and Stickley's proud moral philosophy (adumbrated in the introductions to the first catalog in this volume) was being promulgated to receptive minds throughout the country.

But by 1915, when the second of these catalogs appeared, much had changed. A comparison of the two catalogs is striking. The 1912 catalog displays 51 pages of goods, of which all but one consist primarily of furniture and all of that exemplifies the Craftsman style. The 1915 catalog (which actually bears no date) offers 30 pages of goods, only 18 of which consist primarily of furniture and barely three of which represent Stickley's characteristic style. Many of the wares are evidently the work of other firms. There is no introduction to Stickley's philosophy, no advertisement for the Craftsman homes and none for the magazine.

It was apparently his last catalog; in March 1915 he filed for bankruptcy. The stunning swiftness of the company's decline seems to have had at least two causes. In 1913 Stickley had built a grand twelve-story headquarters in New

York City, in the process seriously overreaching himself financially. At the same time, the public taste for the Craftsman style had peaked and was beginning to wane. In the political realm, the passing of the rugged populism of William Jennings Bryan and Teddy Roosevelt and the advent of the urbane William Howard Taft and Woodrow Wilson roughly paralleled this change of mood. Other companies less firmly linked in the public mind to a particular style found it easier to shift gears, whereas Stickley's adoption of a variety of new styles must have been merely confusing.

By the time of his death decades later, Stickley was a forgotten figure. But his ideals and those of his kindred spirits—Ernest Thompson Seton, John Burroughs, Jack London, Louis Sullivan, Arthur Farwell, to name a few— marked a generation. His furniture—timeless, comfortable and built to last— still fills countless homes and cottages, exerting its benign influence, as Stickley had hoped, long after the ephemera of its time have vanished.

For further reading: Important books on the whole movement include Robert Judson Clark's exhibition catalog *The Arts and Crafts Movement in America, 1876–1916* (Princeton, N.J.: Art Museum, Princeton University, & Art Institute of Chicago, c.1972), Peter Davey's *Architecture of the Arts and Crafts Movement* (New York: Rizzoli, c.1980), Gillian Naylor's *The Arts and Crafts Movement* (Cambridge, Mass.: MIT Press, 1980) and Wendy Kaplan's *"The Art That Is Life": The Arts and Crafts Movement in America, 1875–1920* (Boston: Museum of Fine Arts & Little, Brown, 1987). Mary Ann Smith is the author of Stickley's biography, *Gustav Stickley, the Craftsman* (Syracuse, N.Y.: Syracuse University Press, 1983). Stickley's 1910 furniture catalog has been reprinted in *Stickley Craftsman Furniture Catalogs* (New York: Dover, 1979). Furniture plans from *The Craftsman* have been collected in *Making Authentic Craftsman Furniture* (Dover, 1986), and similar collections of house plans are available in *Craftsman Homes, More Craftsman Homes* and *Craftsman Bungalows* (Dover, 1979, 1981, 1988).

CRAFTSMAN
FURNITURE

APRIL
1912

MADE BY

GUSTAV STICKLEY

AT THE CRAFTSMAN WORKSHOPS
EASTWOOD, N.Y.

SHOW ROOMS:
29 WEST 34TH ST., NEW YORK   470 BOYLSTON ST., BOSTON

"CRAFTSMAN"

TRADE
MARKS
REG'D

IN U.S.
PATENT
OFFICE

"Stickley"

HOW TO IDENTIFY CRAFTSMAN FURNITURE

Each piece of Craftsman furniture bears my shop-mark shown above—joiner's compasses enclosing the motto *Als ik kan*, and the written signature "Stickley," both of which are trade-marks registered in the United States Patent Office.

Among those who are imitating my styles are other furniture-makers named Stickley. Purchasers, therefore, should always look for the word "Craftsman"—also a registered trade-mark—on the tags and pasters attached to each piece of my furniture.

The joiner's compasses, a primitive cabinetmaker's tool, are symbolic of the fundamental principles on which my furniture is based, and the motto, *Als ik kan*, taken from the Flemish and meaning "As I can," recalls the old-time craftsman ideals of earnest and thorough workmanship.

My furniture is made at The Craftsman Workshops, Eastwood, N. Y., and I have no connection with any other factory. Each piece of furniture before it leaves the factory is provided with a tag which carrries the price at which the piece is to be sold in the store. Cost of transportation necessitates two price lists, one for Eastern and one for far Western States.

GUSTAV STICKLEY
THE CRAFTSMAN WORKSHOPS, EASTWOOD, N. Y.
SHOW ROOMS.
29 WEST 34th ST , NEW YORK CITY   470 BOYLSTON ST., BOSTON.

ORDER NUMBER OF THIS PIECE OF FURNITURE IS _____

Form of paster which will hereafter be attached to each piece of Craftsman furniture.

CRAFTSMAN FURNITURE

LIVING ROOM IN HOME OF MR. R. M. BOND, DE LAND, FLORIDA, WITH CRAFTSMAN FURNISHINGS.

MADE BY

GUSTAV STICKLEY

AT THE CRAFTSMAN WORKSHOPS

EASTWOOD, N.Y. (P.O. ADDRESS-SYRACUSE, N.Y.)

SHOW ROOMS:

29 WEST 34TH ST., NEW YORK   470 BOYLSTON ST., BOSTON

GUSTAV STICKLEY: ORIGINATOR OF CRAFTSMAN HOUSES AND CRAFTSMAN FURNITURE: FOUNDER AND EDITOR OF THE CRAFTSMAN MAGAZINE.

WHAT CRAFTSMAN FURNITURE STANDS FOR

WITHIN the last twelve years the popularity of Craftsman furniture has increased so largely that it is now recognized as a national style. This is partly because it was intended primarily to fill, in the most direct and natural way, the actual needs of American home life, and partly because at the time it was put forward people were on the verge of an artistic awakening, a reaction against the insincerity and false ornateness of the furnishings of that period. The impetus of this movement, being in the direction of my own efforts, naturally helped to carry my work forward to success.

Today the word "Craftsman" has become established in the public mind as a synonym for simple, well-made furniture, constructed on primitive lines, planned for comfort, durability and beauty, and expressing the spirit of true democracy.

The original pieces of Craftsman furniture were made in 1898. For two years I experimented and worked over the many problems of design, construction and finishing. In 1900 I exhibited my first Craftsman furniture to the general public at the Furniture Exposition in Grand Rapids, Michigan, with decidedly encouraging results. The following year it was again shown at the Pan-American Exposition, and from that time it found a welcome in the homes of the people.

Then there developed the making of the various furniture accessories—strong simple hinges, handles and pulls of iron, copper and brass. I also found that I needed just the right sort of leather and fabrics for cushions, table tops and chair seats, and so I studied and experimented with these materials until I discovered the sort of treatment they required to bring them into harmony with my furniture.

As the use of Craftsman furniture offered such interesting opportunities to develop an entire decorative scheme along the same lines, I gradually branched out from the metal and upholstery work into the making of electric lighting fixtures, lamps, candlesticks, fireplace fittings, trays, etc., and also curtains, portières, pillows, scarfs, centerpieces, with simple designs and colorings.

In all these things I have tried to get the best possible results, using only suitable materials and the best workmanship. I try always to work *with* the material rather than to force it to my own ends, to retain and emphasize the natural interest of grain, texture and color. For instance, the oak finish which I use has been fumed and finished in a way that preserves the inherent beauties of the wood, with just enough color added to heighten the original effect. This finish, in fact, which I have worked so long to attain, is now recognized as the standard finish for which everyone is striving.

Most of my furniture was so carefully designed and well-proportioned in the first place, that even with my advanced experience I cannot improve upon it. Month by month, of course, I am adding new pieces to fill some special need, but there are few changes in the original designs. For this reason, people who are buying Craftsman furniture can feel that the pieces they purchase today will never go "out of style," but will be even more appropriate and beautiful as time goes on.

A number of such new designs are included in the following pages, and to all who are interested I extend a cordial invitation to visit the show rooms in New York or other cities. (A list of my associates will be found on the inside of the back cover.) I feel sure that the use of Craftsman furniture will continue to increase from year to year, for the reason that it provides the kind of home environment most suited to the real needs of our American democracy. And I care so much about the things I make that I want people to be happy with them.

HOW TO IDENTIFY CRAFTSMAN FURNITURE

"CRAFTSMAN"

TRADE MARKS REG'D

IN U.S. PATENT OFFICE

"Stickley"

THE success of my furniture has given rise to many imitations, as well as to the too free application of the word "Craftsman." There is but one make of Craftsman furniture, and purchasers who wish to obtain the genuine should remember its very simple means of identification.

Every piece of furniture bears the word "Craftsman," with my shop-mark—joiners' compasses, enclosing the motto *Als ik kan*—and the written signature "Stickley," all of which trade-marks are registered in the United States Patent Office.

In order to get the benefit of my work and reputation, imitators get as close to my trade-marks as they dare legally, and although such imitation is complimentary in a certain sense, it is apt to be misleading. To avoid, therefore, any possibility of confusion with other so-called "Stickley furniture"—for among the imitators are those who bear the same name as myself—it is well for purchasers to look always for the word "Craftsman" which appears on the tags and pasters attached to each piece that I make.

The Craftsman Workshops, where my furniture is made, are at Eastwood, N. Y., and I have no connection with any other factory. Each piece of furniture, before it leaves the factory, is provided with a tag which carries the price at which the piece is to be sold in the store. Owing to the cost of transportation across the continent, it is necessary to have two price lists, one for the Eastern and one for far Western States.

On the inside of the front cover of this catalogue is a form of paster which will hereafter be pasted to the furniture—usually underneath, as under the seat of a chair, beneath the top of a table or in a drawer. This paster carries the trade-marks previously referred to. I chose this motto and sign as a permanent means of identification for my furniture because they seemed to me to embody best the spirit and purpose of my work. The joiner's compasses, being one of the first and simplest of the cabinetmaker's tools, are symbolic not only of my craft, but also of my own attitude toward it; for it has been my aim to express fundamental principles in both design and workmanship, and to make furniture primarily strong, durable and comfortable, and to base whatever beauty might be attained upon sound structural qualities and the natural interest of the materials used. The motto—*Als ik kan* (as I can)—which originated with one of the Flemish painters of the fourteenth century, Ian van Eyck, reflects that sentiment of courage and persistency which characterized the artists and craftsmen of the olden times, when a man's work whether manual or intellectual was held to be the noblest source of inspiration, growth and pride. It was this same legend that William Morris used, in its French form, *Si je puis*, after his visit to the Low Countries fired his enthusiasm for good craftsmanship. Its application to Craftsman furniture recalls the old-time ideals of thoroughness of workmanship, and expresses the earnestness of my endeavor to help put the art of furniture-making once more on a sound and sincere basis.

Gustav Stickley

No. 338
CHAR $6.50
RUSH OR SOFT LEATHER SLIP SEAT
BACK 40 IN. HIGH.   SEAT 18 IN. HIGH, 15 IN.
WIDE, 16 IN. DEEP

No. 340
ARM CHAIR $10.00
RUSH OR SOFT LEATHER SLIP SEAT
BACK 41 IN. HIGH.   SEAT 18 IN. HIGH, 20 IN.
WIDE, 16 IN. DEEP

338

340

339

337

No. 339
ARM ROCKER . $10.00
RUSH OR SOFT LEATHER
SLIP SEAT
BACK 36 IN. HIGH. SEAT
15 IN. HIGH, 18 IN. WIDE,
16 IN. DEEP

No. 337
ROCKER . . . $6.50
RUSH OR SOFT LEATHER
SLIP SEAT
BACK 35 IN. HIGH.   SEAT
14 IN. HIGH, 15 IN. WIDE,
16 IN. DEEP

No. 370
CHAIR $7.00
RUSH OR SOFT LEATHER SLIP SEAT
BACK 36 IN. HIGH.   SEAT 18 IN. HIGH, 17 IN.
WIDE, 16 IN. DEEP

No. 370-A
ARM CHAIR $11.00
RUSH OR SOFT LEATHER SLIP SEAT
BACK 36 IN. HIGH.   SEAT 18 IN. HIGH, 20 IN.
WIDE, 18 IN. DEEP

370

370-A

No. 309½

ARM ROCKER $10.50
HARD LEATHER SEAT
BACK 32 IN. HIGH
SEAT 15 IN. HIGH, 20 IN. WIDE, 19 IN. DEEP

No. 309 (SAME DESIGN AND SIZE AS 309½)
ARM ROCKER, RUSH SEAT $9.00

No. 305½

ROCKER $6.50
HARD LEATHER SEAT
BACK 31 IN. HIGH
SEAT 14 IN. HIGH, 16 IN. WIDE, 16 IN. DEEP

No. 305 (SAME DESIGN AND SIZE AS 305½)
ROCKER, RUSH SEAT $5.50

309½

305½

No. 306½

CHAIR . . . $6.50
HARD LEATHER SEAT
BACK 36 IN. HIGH. SEAT
18 IN. HIGH, 16 IN. WIDE,
16 IN. DEEP

No. 306 (SAME DESIGN
AND DIMENSIONS AS 306½)
CHAIR, RUSH SEAT $5.50

No. 350

CHAIR . . . $7.00
HARD LEATHER SEAT
BACK 39 IN. HIGH. SEAT
18 IN. HIGH, 16 IN. WIDE
16 IN. DEEP

No. 350-A

ARM CHAIR . $10.75
(FOR DESCRIPTION SEE
PRICE LIST)

306½

310½

No. 310½

ARM CHAIR . $10.50
HARD LEATHER SEAT
BACK 36 IN. HIGH. SEAT
18 IN. HIGH, 20 IN. WIDE
19 IN. DEEP

No. 310 (SAME SIZE
AND DIMENSIONS AS 310½)
ARM CHAIR,
RUSH SEAT . $9.00

No. 365

ARM ROCKER . $11.00
HARD LEATHER SEAT
BACK 38 IN HIGH. SEAT
15 IN. HIGH, 20 IN. WIDE
17 IN. DEEP

No. 366

ARM CHAIR . $11.00
HARD LEATHER SEAT
BACK 39 IN HIGH. SEAT
18 IN. HIGH, 20 IN. WIDE
17 IN. DEEP

350

366

365

379

No. 329

CHAIR, SHEEPSKIN CUSHION $9.50
SOFT LEATHER CUSHION $10.50
BACK 32 IN. HIGH. SEAT 16 IN. HIGH, 17 IN.
WIDE, 15 IN. DEEP

380

329

No. 379

ROCKER, LOOSE SEAT CUSHION,
SHEEPSKIN $10.00
SOFT LEATHER . . . $11.00
BACK 32 IN. HIGH. SEAT 14 IN.
HIGH, 17½ IN. WIDE, 16 IN.
DEEP

No. 380

CHAIR, LOOSE SEAT CUSHION,
SHEEPSKIN $10.00
SOFT LEATHER . . . $11.00
BACK 37 IN. HIGH. SEAT 18 IN.
HIGH, 17½ IN. WIDE, 16 IN.
DEEP

303

No. 397

ARM ROCKER, SPRING
SEAT CUSHION, SHEEP-
SKIN $14.50
SOFT LEATHER . $15.50
BACK 43 IN. HIGH. SEAT
15 IN. HIGH, 20 IN. WIDE,
18 IN. DEEP.

No. 303

ROCKER, SPRING SEAT
CUSHION,
SHEEPSKIN . $10.00
SOFT LEATHER $11.00
BACK 33 IN. HIGH
SEAT 14 IN. HIGH, 17
IN. WIDE, 16 IN. DEEP

387

No. 387

ROCKER, SPRING SEAT CUSHION, SHEEPSKIN . . . $10.50
SOFT LEATHER $11.50
BACK 42 IN. HIGH. SEAT 15 IN. HIGH, 17 IN. WIDE, 18 IN. DEEP

397

TRADE-
MARK
REG'D
IN U.S.
PATENT
OFFICE

349½

349½A

No. 312½B

BILLIARD CHAIR . . . $13.50
HARD LEATHER SEAT
BACK 46 IN. HIGH. SEAT 26 IN.
HIGH, 21 IN. WIDE, 18 IN. DEEP

312½B

No. 349½
CHAIR $8.00
HARD LEATHER SEAT
BACK 38 IN. HIGH. SEAT 18
IN. HIGH, 18 IN. WIDE, 16½
IN. DEEP

No. 349½A
ARM CHAIR . . . $12.00
HARD LEATHER SEAT
BACK 38 IN. HIGH. SEAT 18
IN. HIGH, 22 IN. WIDE, 19 IN.
DEEP.

No. 311½
ARM ROCKER . . . $12.50
HARD LEATHER SEAT
BACK 34 IN. HIGH. SEAT 15
IN. HIGH, 20 IN. WIDE, 19 IN.
DEEP

No. 311
(SAME DESIGN AND SIZE AS
311½)
ARM ROCKER,
RUSH SEAT . . . $11.00

354½

No. 312½
ARM CHAIR $12.50
BACK 37 IN. HIGH. SEAT 18 IN.
HIGH, 20 IN. WIDE, 19 IN. DEEP

No. 312
(SAME DESIGN AND SIZE AS 312½)
ARM CHAIR, RUSH SEAT . $11.00

311½

No. 354½
CHAIR $8.50
HARD LEATHER SEAT
BACK 36 IN. HIGH. SEAT 18 IN.
HIGH, 18 IN. WIDE, 16 IN. DEEP

No. 354½A
ARM CHAIR $12.50
(FOR DESCRIPTION SEE PRICE LIST)

312½

TRADE IN U.S.
MARK PATENT
REG'D OFFICE

314 313

No. 398
CHAIR . . $4.50
RUSH OR SOFT
LEATHER SLIP SEAT
BACK 32 IN. HIGH
SEAT 18 IN. HIGH, 17
IN. WIDE, 15 IN. DEEP

No. 313
ARM ROCKER . $9.00
RUSH OR SOFT
LEATHER SLIP SEAT
BACK 38 IN. HIGH
SEAT 15 IN. HIGH, 21
IN. WIDE, 18 IN. DEEP

398

No. 314
ARM CHAIR . . . $9.00
RUSH OR SOFT LEATHER SLIP
SEAT
BACK 40 IN. HIGH
SEAT 18 IN. HIGH, 21 IN.
WIDE, 18 IN. DEEP

No. 307
ROCKER $4.75
RUSH OR SOFT LEATHER SLIP
SEAT
BACK 36 IN. HIGH
SEAT 15 IN. HIGH, 17 IN.
WIDE, 15 IN. DEEP

No. 300
STOOL $7.50
HARD LEATHER SEAT
15 IN. HIGH, 20 IN. WIDE,
16 IN. DEEP

307

308

No. 308
CHAIR $4.75
RUSH OR SOFT LEATHER SLIP
SEAT
BACK 40 IN. HIGH
SEAT 18 IN. HIGH, 17 IN.
WIDE, 15 IN. DEEP

No. 301
STOOL $4.50
RUSH SEAT
17 IN. HIGH, 20 IN. WIDE,
16 IN. DEEP

No. 302
FOOT STOOL . . $2.50
HARD LEATHER TOP
5 IN. HIGH, 12 IN. WIDE, 12
IN. DEEP

No. 299
STOOL $4.50
HARD LEATHER TOP
9 IN. HIGH, 16 IN. WIDE, 12
IN. DEEP

300

302

301

299

317

318

No. 317

ARM ROCKER, SPRING SEAT CUSHION

SHEEPSKIN $17.00

SOFT LEATHER $18.00

BACK 38 IN. HIGH

SEAT 15 IN. HIGH, 21 IN. WIDE, 19 IN. DEEP

No. 318

ARM CHAIR, SPRING SEAT CUSHION

SHEEPSKIN $17.00

SOFT LEATHER $18.00

BACK 38 IN. HIGH

SEAT 18 IN. HIGH, 21 IN. WIDE, 19 IN. DEEP

322

322-A

No. 322

CHAIR . . $14.00

HARD LEATHER SEAT

AND BACK

BACK 38 IN. HIGH

SEAT 18 IN. HIGH, 18

IN. WIDE, 16½ IN.

DEEP

No. 322-A

ARM CHAIR . $20.00

HARD LEATHER SEAT

AND BACK

BACK 38 IN. HIGH

SEAT 18 IN. HIGH, 22

IN. WIDE, 19 IN.

DEEP

No. 355

CHAIR $22.50

HARD LEATHER SEAT AND BACK

BACK 33 IN. HIGH

SEAT 18 IN. HIGH, 19 IN. WIDE, 17 IN. DEEP

No. 355-A

ARM CHAIR $32.50

HARD LEATHER SEAT AND BACK

BACK 37 IN. HIGH

SEAT 18 IN. HIGH, 21 IN. WIDE, 20 IN. DEEP

355

355-A

TRADE-   IN U.S.
MARK   PATENT
REG'D   OFFICE

10

335

No. 333
ARM CHAIR, SHEEPSKIN
CUSHIONS $33.00
SOFT LEATHER . . $38.00
BACK 39 IN. HIGH. SEAT 16
IN. HIGH, 23 IN. WIDE, 25 IN.
DEEP

333

No. 335
ARM CHAIR, SHEEPSKIN CUSHIONS . $30.00
SOFT LEATHER $35.00
BACK 30 IN. HIGH
SEAT 16 IN. HIGH, 23
IN. WIDE, 26 IN.
DEEP

No. 381
ARM ROCKER, SHEEP-
SKIN CUSHIONS $18.00
SOFT LEATHER $21.00
BACK 39 IN. HIGH
SEAT 15 IN. HIGH, 19
IN. WIDE, 19 IN.
DEEP

381

382

No. 382
ARM CHAIR, SHEEP-
SKIN CUSHIONS $18.00
SOFT LEATHER $21.00
BACK 39 IN. HIGH
SEAT 18 IN. HIGH,
19 IN. WIDE, 19 IN.
DEEP

No. 371
ARM ROCKER, SHEEPSKIN
CUSHIONS $24.00
SOFT LEATHER $29.00
BACK 36 IN. HIGH. SEAT 15 IN. HIGH,
20½ IN. WIDE, 21½ IN. DEEP

No. 372
ARM CHAIR, SHEEPSKIN CUSHIONS $24.00
SOFT LEATHER $29.00
BACK 39 IN. HIGH. SEAT 16 IN. HIGH,
20½ IN. WIDE, 21½ IN. DEEP.

371

372

No. 319

ARM ROCKER, SPRING
SEAT CUSHION, SHEEP-
SKIN . . $27.00
SOFT LEATHER $32.00
BACK 38 IN. HIGH
SEAT 15 IN. HIGH,
21 IN. WIDE, 25 IN.
DEEP

319

320

No. 320

ARM CHAIR, SPRING
SEAT CUSHION, SHEEP-
SKIN . . $27.00
SOFT LEATHER $32.00
BACK 42 IN. HIGH
SEAT 16 IN. HIGH,
21 IN. WIDE, 25 IN.
DEEP

No. 323

ARM ROCKER, SPRING SEAT
CUSHION, SHEEPSKIN $29.00
SOFT LEATHER $34.00
BACK 40 IN. HIGH
SEAT 15 IN. HIGH, 22 IN.
WIDE, 25 IN. DEEP

No. 347

EASTWOOD CHAIR, SOFT
LEATHER CUSHIONS . $43.00
SHEEPSKIN . . . $38.00
VELOUR $38.00
BACK 37 IN. HIGH
SEAT 16 IN. HIGH, 27 IN.
WIDE, 27 IN. DEEP
ARMS 6 IN. WIDE
POSTS $2\frac{3}{4}$ IN. SQUARE
CANE SEAT

347

No. 324

ARM CHAIR, SPRING SEAT
CUSHION, SHEEPSKIN $29.00
SOFT LEATHER . $34.00
BACK 41 IN. HIGH
SEAT 16 IN. HIGH, 22 IN.
WIDE, 25 IN. DEEP

323

324

TRADE-
MARK
REG'D

IN U.S.
PATENT
OFFICE

No. 396

CHAIR, SPRING SEAT CUSHION
SHEEPSKIN $38.00
SOFT LEATHER $43.00
BACK 41 IN. HIGH.   SEAT 16 IN. HIGH,
23 IN. WIDE, 28 IN. DEEP

336

No. 336

RECLINING CHAIR
ADJUSTABLE BACK
SPRING SEAT CUSHION
SHEEPSKIN . $31.50
SOFT LEATHER $36.50
BACK 40 IN. HIGH
SEAT 16 IN. HIGH, 22
IN. WIDE, 23 IN. DEEP

396

No. 346

RECLINING CHAIR, ADJUSTABLE
BACK, SPRING SEAT CUSHION
SHEEPSKIN $25.50
SOFT LEATHER $30.50
BACK 41 IN. HIGH.   SEAT 16 IN.
HIGH, 21 IN. WIDE, 24 IN. DEEP

346

No. 369

RECLINING CHAIR
ADJUSTABLE BACK
SPRING SEAT CUSHION
SHEEPSKIN . . $37.00
SOFT LEATHER . $42.00
BACK 40 IN. HIGH
SEAT 15 IN. HIGH, 23 IN.
WIDE, 27 IN. DEEP

No. 332

RECLINING CHAIR, ADJUSTABLE
BACK, SPRING SEAT CUSHION
SHEEPSKIN $33.00
SOFT LEATHER $38.00
BACK 40 IN. HIGH.   SEAT 16 IN.
HIGH, 23 IN. WIDE, 27 IN. DEEP

369

332

TRADE-
MARK
REG'D

IN U.S.
PATENT
OFFICE

GUSTAV STICKLEY

225

No. 225
SETTLE $68.00
SPRING SEAT CUSHION
SOFT LEATHER
BACK 29 IN. HIGH
SEAT 16 IN. HIGH, 79 IN.
LONG, 31 IN. DEEP
PILLOWS EXTRA
SHEEPSKIN EACH . . $8.00
SOFT LEATHER EACH $10.00

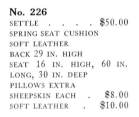

No. 226
SETTLE $50.00
SPRING SEAT CUSHION
SOFT LEATHER
BACK 29 IN. HIGH
SEAT 16 IN. HIGH, 60 IN.
LONG, 30 IN. DEEP
PILLOWS EXTRA
SHEEPSKIN EACH . $8.00
SOFT LEATHER . $10.00

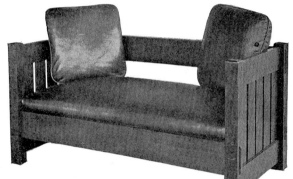

226

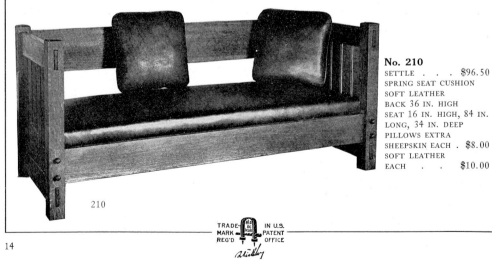

No. 210
SETTLE . . . $96.50
SPRING SEAT CUSHION
SOFT LEATHER
BACK 36 IN. HIGH
SEAT 16 IN. HIGH, 84 IN.
LONG, 34 IN. DEEP
PILLOWS EXTRA
SHEEPSKIN EACH . $8.00
SOFT LEATHER
EACH . . $10.00

210

TRADE- IN U.S.
MARK PATENT
REG'D OFFICE
Stickley

No. 208

SETTLE $78.00
SPRING SEAT CUSHION, SOFT
LEATHER
BACK 29 IN. HIGH
SEAT 16 IN. HIGH, 76 IN.
LONG, 32 IN. DEEP
PILLOWS EXTRA
SHEEPSKIN, EACH . $8.00
SOFT LEATHER, EACH $10.00

208

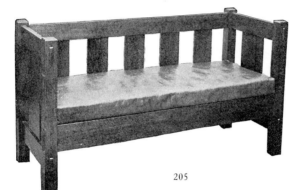

No. 205

SETTLE $35.00
SPRING SEAT CUSHION, SOFT
LEATHER
BACK 30 IN. HIGH
SEAT 16 IN. HIGH, 56 IN.
LONG, 22 IN. DEEP

205

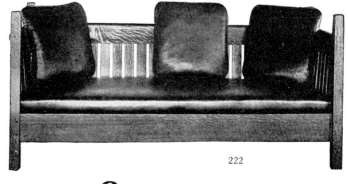

No. 222

SETTLE $90.00
SPRING SEAT CUSHION, SOFT
LEATHER
BACK 36 IN. HIGH
SEAT 16 IN. HIGH, 80 IN.
LONG, 33 IN. DEEP
PILLOWS EXTRA
SHEEPSKIN, EACH . $8.00
SOFT LEATHER, EACH $10.00

222

15

GUSTAV STICKLEY

No. 216
SETTLE $58.00
SPRING SEAT CUSHION, SOFT
LEATHER
ENDS 29 IN. HIGH
SEAT 16 IN. HIGH, 79 IN.
LONG, 31 IN. WIDE
PILLOWS EXTRA
SHEEPSKIN, EACH . $8.00
SOFT LEATHER, EACH $10.00

216

212

No. 212
SETTLE $25.00
HARD LEATHER SEAT
BACK 36 IN. HIGH
SEAT 18 IN. HIGH, 48 IN. LONG, 21 IN.
DEEP

No. 218
(SAME DESIGN AS 219)
SETTLE $35.00
SPRING SEAT CUSHION, SOFT LEATHER
BACK 39 IN. HIGH
SEAT 18 IN. HIGH, 48 IN. LONG, 23 IN.
DEEP

No. 219
SETTLE $45.00
SPRING SEAT CUSHION, SOFT
LEATHER
BACK 39 IN. HIGH
SEAT 18 IN. HIGH, 72 IN.
LONG, 23 IN. DEEP

219

TRADE-MARK REG'D IN U.S. PATENT OFFICE

224

No. 605
TELEPHONE
STAND . . $5.50
29 IN. HIGH
TOP 14 IN. X 14 IN.

No. 224
SEAT $32.00
BACK 42 IN. HIGH. SEAT 17 IN. HIGH, 48 IN. LONG, 20 IN. DEEP
THE SEAT LIFTS, FORMING A BOX WHICH IS 45 IN. LONG AND
8 IN. DEEP

605

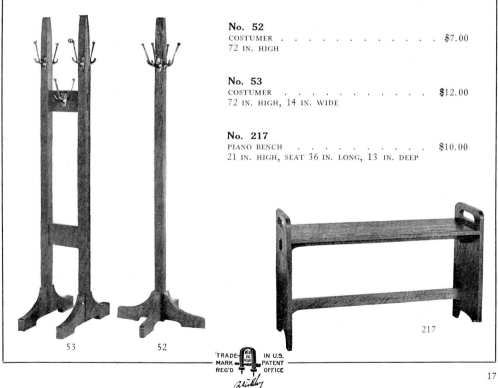

No. 52
COSTUMER $7.00
72 IN. HIGH

No. 53
COSTUMER $12.00
72 IN. HIGH, 14 IN. WIDE

No. 217
PIANO BENCH $10.00
21 IN. HIGH, SEAT 36 IN. LONG, 13 IN. DEEP

53   52

217

GUSTAV STICKLEY

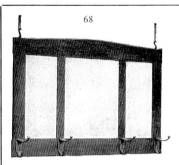

68

66

No. 66
MIRROR $16.00
28 IN. X 36 IN.
GLASS 20 IN. X 30. IN.
IRON HOOKS

No. 910
MIRROR $7.50
29 IN. X 23 IN.
GLASS 26 IN. X 20 IN.

No. 68
MIRROR . . . $21.00
28 IN. X 48 IN.
END GLASS 9 IN. X 20 IN.
CENTER GLASS 20 IN. X 20 IN.
IRON HOOKS

No. 67
(SAME DESIGN AS 68)
MIRROR . . . $18.75
28 IN. X 42 IN.
END GLASS 9 IN. X 20 IN.
CENTER GLASS 16 IN. X 20 IN.
IRON HOOKS
CHAINS AND HOOKS INCLUD-
ED IN ABOVE PRICES

910

No. 100
UMBRELLA STAND . $6.00
24 IN. HIGH
DIAMETER AT TOP 12 IN.
DIAMETER AT BASE 9 IN.
WROUGHT IRON HOOPS
COPPER PAN

No. 54
UMBRELLA STAND . $5.00
29 IN. HIGH
12 IN. SQUARE
COPPER PAN

No. 55
UMBRELLA STAND . $7.00
29 IN. HIGH
21 IN. LONG
12 IN. DEEP
COPPER PAN

55

54

100

TRADE-
MARK
REG'D
IN U.S.
PATENT
OFFICE

No. 91
SCREEN $26.00
SHEEPSKIN PANELS
68 IN. HIGH
THREE PANELS EACH 22 IN. WIDE

No. 702
NEWEL POST LAMP IN COPPER
OR BRASS $12.00
IRON $10.50
LANTERN 8 IN. HIGH
BASE 4 IN. SQUARE
AMBER TINTED HAMMERED
GLASS

702

91

No. 83
SCREEN, PANELED IN JAPANESE GRASS CLOTH . $18.00
PANELED IN CRAFTSMAN CANVAS $22.00
66 IN. HIGH.   THREE PANELS EACH 22 IN. WIDE

No. 512
ELECTRIC SCONCE
(SAME DESIGN AND SIZE AS
513, BUT FITTED WITH TWO
LIGHTS)
COPPER OR BRASS . $12.00
IRON $11.00

513

No. 513
ELECTRIC SCONCE, COMPLETE WITH MICA SHADE
COPPER OR BRASS $8.00
IRON $7.50
SCONCE 12 IN. HIGH, 6 IN. WIDE.   PROJECTION OF
BRACKET 6 IN.   BASE OF SHADE 4 IN.

83

GUSTAV STICKLEY

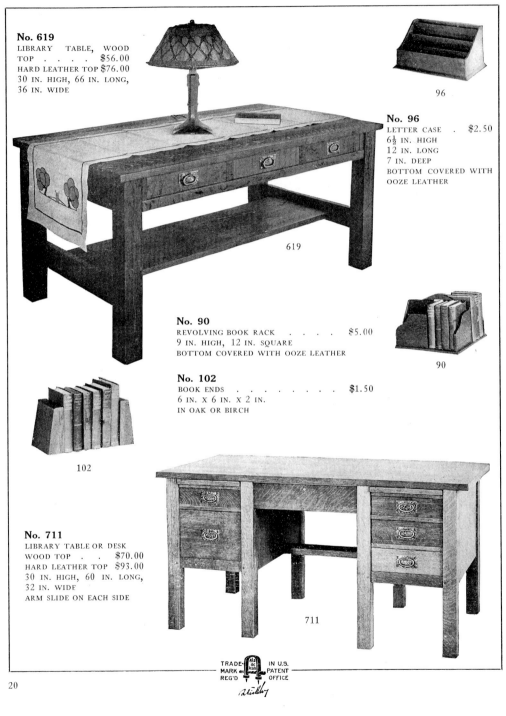

No. 619
LIBRARY TABLE, WOOD
TOP $56.00
HARD LEATHER TOP $76.00
30 IN. HIGH, 66 IN. LONG,
36 IN. WIDE

No. 96
LETTER CASE . $2.50
6½ IN. HIGH
12 IN. LONG
7 IN. DEEP
BOTTOM COVERED WITH
OOZE LEATHER

96

619

No. 90
REVOLVING BOOK RACK $5.00
9 IN. HIGH, 12 IN. SQUARE
BOTTOM COVERED WITH OOZE LEATHER

90

No. 102
BOOK ENDS $1.50
6 IN. X 6 IN. X 2 IN.
IN OAK OR BIRCH

102

No. 711
LIBRARY TABLE OR DESK
WOOD TOP . . $70.00
HARD LEATHER TOP $93.00
30 IN. HIGH, 60 IN. LONG,
32 IN. WIDE
ARM SLIDE ON EACH SIDE

711

TRADE   IN U.S.
MARK   PATENT
REG'D   OFFICE

661

No. 661
LIBRARY
TABLE . . $38.00
30 IN. HIGH, 54 IN. LONG,
32 IN. WIDE

No. 616
LIBRARY TABLE, WOOD TOP . $42.00
HARD LEATHER TOP . . . $58.50
30 IN. HIGH, 54 IN. LONG, 32 IN. WIDE

No. 615
(SAME DESIGN AS 616)
LIBRARY TABLE, WOOD TOP . $35.00
HARD LEATHER TOP . . . $49.00
30 IN. HIGH, 48 IN. LONG, 30 IN. WIDE

614

616

No. 614
LIBRARY TABLE, WOOD TOP . $26.00
HARD LEATHER TOP . . . 38.50
30 IN. HIGH, 42 IN. LONG, 30 IN. WIDE

No. 613
(SAME DESIGN AS 614)
LIBRARY TABLE $19.00
30 IN. HIGH, 36 IN. LONG, 24 IN. WIDE

No. 60
SLIDING
BOOK RACK $2.50
CLOSED 12 IN. LONG
OPEN 18 IN. LONG
INSIDE 7 IN. WIDE

60

TRADE-
MARK
REG'D

IN U.S.
PATENT
OFFICE

GUSTAV STICKLEY

No. 72
MAGAZINE
CABINET
$12.00
42 IN. HIGH
22 IN. WIDE
13 IN. DEEP

72

No. 715
BOOKCASE . . $30.00
ONE DOOR
STATIONARY SHELVES ON
LINE WITH MULLINS
56 IN. HIGH
36 IN. WIDE
13 IN. DEEP

No. 715½
BOOKCASE . . $21.50
SINGLE, 56 IN. HIGH
36 IN. WIDE,
13 IN. DEEP

715

No. 716½
BOOKSHELF
$25.00
DOUBLE
56 IN. HIGH
42 IN. WIDE
13 IN. DEEP

No. 717½
BOOKSHELF
$27.50
DOUBLE
56 IN. HIGH
48 IN. WIDE
13 IN. DEEP

No. 718½
BOOKSHELF
$30.00
DOUBLE
56 IN. HIGH
54 IN. WIDE
13 IN. DEEP

No. 719½
BOOKSHELF
$32.50
DOUBLE
56 IN. HIGH
60 IN. WIDE
13 IN. DEEP

BOOKCASES WITHOUT DOORS
HAVE ADJUSTABLE SHELVES

716½

715½

TRADE MARK REG'D / IN U.S. PATENT OFFICE

523

74

No. 74
BOOK RACK $6.00
31 IN. HIGH, 30 IN. WIDE, 10 IN. DEEP

No. 523
BOOKCASE $26.00
TWO DOORS, STATIONARY SHELVES ON LINE OF
MULLIONS
44 IN. HIGH, 39 IN. WIDE, 12 IN. DEEP

No. 79
MAGAZINE CABINET . $8.50
40 IN. HIGH, 14 IN. WIDE,
10 IN. DEEP

No. 716
BOOKCASE . . . $37.00
TWO DOORS
STATIONARY SHELVES ON
LINE OF MULLIONS
56 IN. HIGH, 42 IN. WIDE,
13 IN. DEEP

No. 717
BOOKCASE . . . $41.00
56 IN. HIGH, 48 IN. WIDE,
13 IN. DEEP

No. 718
BOOKCASE . . . $45.00
56 IN. HIGH, 54 IN. WIDE,
13 IN. DEEP

No. 719
BOOKCASE . . . $49.00
56 IN. HIGH, 60 IN. WIDE,
13 IN. DEEP

79

716

TRADE-MARK REG'D IN U.S. PATENT OFFICE

GUSTAV STICKLEY

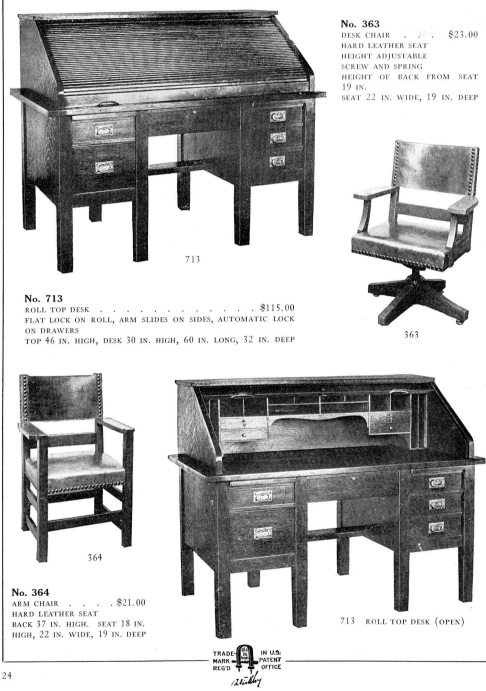

No. 363
DESK CHAIR . . . $23.00
HARD LEATHER SEAT
HEIGHT ADJUSTABLE
SCREW AND SPRING
HEIGHT OF BACK FROM SEAT
19 IN.
SEAT 22 IN. WIDE, 19 IN. DEEP

713

No. 713
ROLL TOP DESK $115.00
FLAT LOCK ON ROLL, ARM SLIDES ON SIDES, AUTOMATIC LOCK
ON DRAWERS
TOP 46 IN. HIGH, DESK 30 IN. HIGH, 60 IN. LONG, 32 IN. DEEP

363

364

No. 364
ARM CHAIR $21.00
HARD LEATHER SEAT
BACK 37 IN. HIGH. SEAT 18 IN.
HIGH, 22 IN. WIDE, 19 IN. DEEP

713   ROLL TOP DESK (OPEN)

162

No. 362
DESK CHAIR $17.00
HARD LEATHER SEAT AND BACK
HEIGHT ADJUSTABLE
SCREW AND SPRING, HEIGHT
OF BACK FROM SEAT 19 IN.
SEAT
18 IN. WIDE
16 IN. DEEP

712

SEE PRICE LIST FOR NUMBER 710

No. 709
DESK, WOOD TOP $38.00
HARD LEATHER
TOP $48.00
29 IN. HIGH, 42 IN. LONG
24 IN. WIDE

No. 360
ARM CHAIR . $18.00
HARD LEATHER SEAT AND
BACK
BACK 37 IN. HIGH
SEAT 18 IN. HIGH
21 IN. WIDE, 18 IN. DEEP

709

No. 94
SCRAP BASKET . $4.75
WROUGHT IRON HOOPS
14 IN. HIGH
DIAMETER AT TOP 12 IN.

No. 712
DESK WITH CABINET
TOP $90.00
30 IN. HIGH, 60 IN. LONG
32 IN. DEEP
ARM SLIDE ON EACH SIDE
CABINETS 6 IN. HIGH
18 IN. LONG, 12 IN. DEEP

No. 361
DESK CHAIR . $23.00
HARD LEATHER SEAT AND
BACK
HEIGHT ADJUSTABLE
SCREW AND SPRING
HEIGHT OF BACK FROM
SEAT 19 IN. SEAT 21 IN.
WIDE, 18 IN. DEEP

94

360

361

TRADE MARK REG'D IN U.S. PATENT OFFICE

25

GUSTAV STICKLEY

729
(CLOSED)

729
(OPEN)

No 729

DESK $39.00
43 IN. HIGH, 36 IN. WIDE, 14 IN. DEEP
WRITING SPACE 34 IN. WIDE, 18 IN. DEEP

No. 732

DESK . . $32.00
42 IN. HIGH,
32 IN. WIDE, 14 IN. DEEP
WRITING SPACE
30 IN. WIDE, 20 IN. DEEP

732
(CLOSED)

732
(OPEN)

TRADE- IN U.S.
MARK PATENT
REG'D OFFICE

No. 728

DESK $20.00
39 IN. HIGH, 30 IN. WIDE, 14 IN. DEEP
WRITING SPACE 27½ IN. WIDE, 21½ IN. DEEP

728
(OPEN)

728
(CLOSED)

731
(OPEN)

731
(CLOSED)

No. 731

DESK $28.00
42 IN. HIGH, 30 IN. WIDE
15 IN. DEEP
WRITING SPACE, 27½ IN. WIDE
23 IN. DEEP

GUSTAV STICKLEY

No. 706
DESK . $26.00
44 IN. HIGH
30 IN. WIDE
11 IN. DEEP
WRITING
SPACE
23 IN. WIDE
17 IN. DEEP

706
(CLOSED)

706
(OPEN)

No. 708
DESK $25.00
30 IN. HIGH, 40 IN. WIDE
22 IN. DEEP
SHELF 8 IN. DEEP
CABINET 6 IN. HIGH, 5 IN. DEEP

No. 720
DESK . . $24.50
30 IN. HIGH
38 IN. WIDE
23 IN. DEEP.
CABINET 8 IN. DEEP
8 IN. HIGH

TRADE-
MARK
REG'D

IN U.S.
PATENT
OFFICE

89

No. 721

DESK . . . $12.00
TOP 38 IN. HIGH
DESK 29 IN. HIGH
CLOSED 13 IN. DEEP
OPEN 23 IN. DEEP

No. 89

SMOKER'S CABINET $12.00
29 IN. HIGH, 20 IN. WIDE, 15 IN. DEEP

721

No. 70W

MUSIC CABINET
PANELED DOOR $20.00
46 IN. HIGH
20 IN. WIDE
16 IN. DEEP
ADJUSTABLE SHELVES

No. 70G

MUSIC CABINET
AMBER GLASS
DOOR. . . $24.00
46 IN. HIGH
20 IN. WIDE
16 IN. DEEP
STATIONARY SHELVES
ON LINE OF MULLIONS

70W

70G

TRADE-MARK REG'D IN U.S. PATENT OFFICE

GUSTAV STICKLEY

50

624

74

No. 74
CANDLESTICK $2.50
9 IN. HIGH
DIAMETER OF SAUCER 7½ IN.
DIAMETER OF SHAFT 1½ IN.

No. 50
COPPER LAMP $18.50
21 IN. HIGH.   DIAMETER AT BASE 7 IN.
THREE LIGHTS AND PULL CHAIN

No. 624
LIBRARY TABLE, WOOD TOP $41.50
HARD LEATHER TOP $58.50
29 IN. HIGH.   HEXAGONAL 48 IN.

No. 633
LIBRARY TABLE
WOOD TOP $30.00
HARD LEATHER TOP . . . $48.00
29 IN. HIGH.   DIAMETER 44 IN.

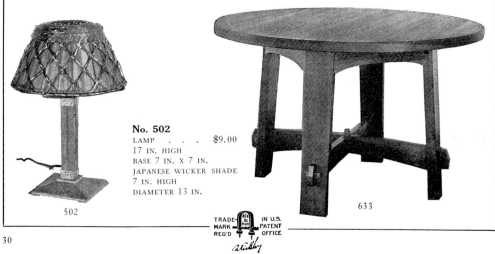

No. 502
LAMP . . . $9.00
17 IN. HIGH
BASE 7 IN. X 7 IN.
JAPANESE WICKER SHADE
7 IN. HIGH
DIAMETER 13 IN.

502

633

No. 656

DINING TABLE

30 IN. HIGH, 48 IN. TOP TO EXTEND 8 FT. . . $48.00
54 IN. TOP TO EXTEND 10 FT. $62.00
54 IN. TOP TO EXTEND 12 FT. $72.00
60 IN. TOP TO EXTEND 12 FT. $85.00

656

632

No. 632

DINING TABLE

30 IN. HIGH, 48 IN. TOP TO EXTEND 8
FT. $36.00
48 IN. TOP TO EXTEND 10 FT. . . $41.00
54 IN. TOP TO EXTEND 10 FT. . . $47.00
54 IN. TOP TO EXTEND 12 FT. . . $53.00
60 IN. TOP TO EXTEND 12 FT. . . $63.00

No. 634

DINING TABLE

30 IN. HIGH, 54 IN. TOP TO EXTEND 10
FT. $60.00
54 IN. TOP TO EXTEND 12 FT. . $70.00
60 IN. TOP TO EXTEND 12 FT. . $82.00

634

TRADE- MARK REG'D IN U.S. PATENT OFFICE

GUSTAV STICKLEY

No. 623
TABLE . . $35.00
30 IN. HIGH
66 IN. LONG
36 IN. WIDE

No. 622
TABLE . . $42.00
30 IN. HIGH
84 IN. LONG
42 IN. WIDE

No. 631
TABLE . . $70.00
30 IN. HIGH
96 IN. LONG
48 IN. WIDE

No. 631½
(SAME DESIGN AS
631)
TABLE . . $48.00
30 IN. HIGH
72 IN. LONG
36 IN. WIDE

623

622

631

TRADE- IN U.S.
MARK PATENT
REG'D OFFICE

653

649

No. 653
LIBRARY
TABLE . . $20.00
30 IN. HIGH
48 IN. LONG
30 IN. WIDE

No. 650
TABLE . . . $14.00
30 IN. HIGH
36 IN. LONG
24 IN. WIDE

No. 675
TABLE
WOOD TOP . $32.00
HARD LEATHER
TOP $46.00
29 IN. HIGH
48 IN. LONG
30 IN. WIDE

650

No. 649
TABLE . . $10.00
30 IN. HIGH
30 IN. LONG
20 IN. WIDE

No. 652
LIBRARY TABLE . $14.00
30 IN. HIGH
36 IN. LONG
24 IN. WIDE

675

652

677

No. 677

TABLE $20.00
30 IN. HIGH
48 IN. LONG
30 IN. WIDE

No. 637

LIBRARY TABLE
WOOD TOP $25.00
HARD LEATHER TOP . . . $38.00
29 IN. HIGH, 48 IN. LONG, 30 IN. WIDE

637

647

No. 647

LUNCH TABLE $14.00
30 IN. HIGH, 40 IN. LONG, 28 IN. WIDE

No. 651

TABLE
WOOD TOP $24.00
HARD LEATHER TOP . . . $38.00
29 IN. HIGH, 48 IN. LONG, 30 IN. WIDE

651

TRADE MARK REG'D   IN U.S. PATENT OFFICE

No. 673
ROUND DROP-LEAF TABLE . $20.00
29 IN. HIGH
DIAMETER OPEN 44 IN.
CLOSED 44 IN. LONG, 14 IN. WIDE

673

No. 638
DROP-LEAF TABLE $20.00
29 IN. HIGH
TOP OPEN 40 IN. X 42 IN.
TOP CLOSED 40 IN. X 14 IN.

671

No. 671
ROUND DROP-LEAF TABLE . $14.00
29 IN. HIGH
DIAMETER OPEN 32 IN.
CLOSED 32 IN. LONG, 10 IN. WIDE

No. 672
(SAME DESIGN AS 671)
ROUND DROP-LEAF TABLE . $18.00
29 IN. HIGH
DIAMETER OPEN 38 IN.
CLOSED 38 IN. LONG, 12 IN. WIDE

638

TRADE- MARK REG'D IN U.S. PATENT OFFICE

GUSTAV STICKLEY

No. 669
TABLE $23.50
30 IN. HIGH
DIAMETER 50 IN.

669

No. 626
TABLE $19.50
30 IN. HIGH
DIAMETER 40 IN.

626

No. 667
TABLE $13.00
30 IN. HIGH
DIAMETER 38 IN.

No. 668
(SAME DESIGN AS 667)
TABLE $18.00
30 IN. HIGH
DIAMETER 44 IN.

667

TRADE MARK REG'D IN U.S. PATENT OFFICE

No. 644

TABLE $12.00
29 IN. HIGH, DIAMETER 30 IN.

No. 645

(SAME DESIGN AS 644)
TABLE $16.00
29 IN. HIGH, DIAMETER 36 IN.

654

No. 646

(SAME DESIGN AS 644)
TABLE . . . $20.00
29 IN. HIGH
DIAMETER 40 IN.

No. 654

TEA TABLE $6.25
28 IN. HIGH
DIAMETER 24 IN.

644

No. 608

TEA TABLE $7.50
26 IN. HIGH, DIAMETER OF TOP 24 IN.
SHELF 12 IN. HIGH

607

608

No. 607

TABLE $10.00
29 IN. HIGH
DIAMETER 24 IN.

604

No. 604
TEA TABLE $4.75
26 IN. HIGH.   DIAMETER 20 IN.

No. 603
TABOURET $3.75
20 IN. HIGH.   DIAMETER 18 IN.

603

No. 602
TABOURET $3.00
18 IN. HIGH.   DIAMETER 16 IN.

602

601

No. 601
TABOURET . . . $2.50
16 IN. HIGH
DIAMETER 14 IN.

No. 660
PLANT STAND . $4.50
20 IN. HIGH
TOP 18 IN. X 18 IN.

611

No. 611
TABLE $9.00
29 IN. HIGH.   TOP 24 IN. X 24 IN.

660

666

No. 666
TEA TABLE $11.00
24 IN. HIGH
TOP CLOSED 8 IN. X 22 IN.
TOP OPEN 26 IN. X 22 IN.

No. 630
SEWING TABLE . . . $18.50
28 IN. HIGH
TOP CLOSED 18 IN. SQUARE
TOP OPEN 38 IN. X 18 IN.
TOP DRAWER 4 IN. DEEP
LOWER DRAWER 6 IN. DEEP
TOP DRAWER FITTED WITH CEDAR
TRAY

630

No. 638
DROP-LEAF TABLE $20.00
29 IN. HIGH
TOP OPEN 40 IN. X 42 IN.
TOP CLOSED 40 IN. X14 IN.

No. 92
TABLE CABINET . $9.00
9 IN. HIGH, 24 IN. LONG
9 IN. DEEP
BOTTOM COVERED WITH
LEATHER

638

No. 308
CHAIR . . . $4.75
RUSH OR SOFT LEATHER
SEAT
BACK 40 IN. HIGH
SEAT 18 IN. HIGH, 17 IN.
WIDE, 15 IN. DEEP

No. 665
NEST OF TABLES $12.00
LARGE TABLE 29 IN. HIGH
24 IN. LONG, 17 IN. WIDE
CENTER TABLE 28½ IN. HIGH
20½ IN. LONG, 16 IN. WIDE
SMALL TABLE 28 IN. HIGH
17 IN. LONG, 14½ IN. WIDE

95

No. 95
SHIRTWAIST BOX $16.00
16 IN. HIGH, 32 IN. LONG, 17 IN. WIDE
CEDAR LINED
HAND-WROUGHT LIFTS

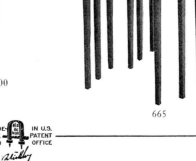

665

TRADE- IN U.S.
MARK PATENT
REG'D OFFICE

814

No. 369

CHAFING DISH, LID, STANDARD AND
TRAY OF HAMMERED COPPER WITH
GLAZED CASSEROLE
PRICE WITH TRAY . . $15.00
CAPACITY OF CASSEROLE 2 QUARTS
DIAMETER OF TRAY 13 IN.

No. 814

SIDEBOARD $68.00
TOP OF PLATE RAIL 49 IN. HIGH
TABLE 38 IN. HIGH, 66 IN. WIDE
24 IN. DEEP
TOP DRAWER LINED WITH OOZE
LEATHER

369

No. 814½

(SAME DESIGN AS 814)
SIDEBOARD . . . $50.00
TOP OF PLATE RAIL 49 IN. HIGH
TABLE 38 IN. HIGH, 56 IN. WIDE
22 IN. DEEP
TOP DRAWER LINED WITH OOZE
LEATHER

No. 817

SIDEBOARD . . . $84.00
TOP OF PLATE RAIL 50 IN. HIGH
TABLE 41 IN. HIGH, 70 IN. WIDE
25 IN. DEEP
TOP DRAWER LINED WITH OOZE
LEATHER

817

TRADE MARK REG'D — IN U.S. PATENT OFFICE

No. 816.

SIDEBOARD $34.00

TOP OF PLATE RAIL 48 IN. HIGH

TABLE 38 IN. HIGH, 48 IN. WIDE 18 IN. DEEP

TOP SMALL DRAWER LINED WITH OOZE LEATHER

816

No. 819

SIDEBOARD $28.00

39 IN. HIGH, 48 IN. WIDE, 20 IN. DEEP

CENTER DRAWER LINED WITH OOZE LEATHER

819

No. 802

SERVING TABLE $18.00

38 IN. HIGH, 42 IN. WIDE, 18 IN. DEEP

802

TRADE- MARK REG'D   IN U.S. PATENT OFFICE

GUSTAV STICKLEY

818

No. 818
SERVING TABLE $22.00
39 IN. HIGH, 48 IN. WIDE, 20 IN. DEEP
CENTER DRAWER LINED WITH OOZE LEATHER

No. 815
CHINA CABINET $45.00
65 IN. HIGH, 42 IN. WIDE, 15 IN. DEEP
THREE STATIONARY SHELVES ON LINE OF MULLIONS

No. 820
CHINA CABINET $32.00
60 IN. HIGH, 36 IN. WIDE, 15 IN. DEEP
GLASS SIDES, STATIONARY SHELVES ON LINE OF
MULLIONS

820

815

No. 822
(DESIGN SIMILAR TO 815 BUT WITH SINGLE DOOR)
CHINA CABINET $30.00
58 IN. HIGH, 36 IN. WIDE, 13 IN. DEEP

914

911

912

No. 914

TOILET TABLE $26.00
TOP OF MIRROR 55 IN. HIGH
TABLE 30 IN. HIGH, 36 IN. WIDE, 18 IN. DEEP
GLASS 20 IN. X 24 IN
WOOD KNOBS

No. 911

DRESSER $50.00
TOP OF MIRROR 66 IN. HIGH, TABLE 33 IN. HIGH
48 IN. WIDE, 22 IN. DEEP
GLASS 28 IN. X 34 IN. WOOD KNOBS

No. 912

BED $30.00
HEADBOARD 51 IN. HIGH,
LENGTH 75 IN. (INSIDE)
WIDTH 54 IN. (INSIDE)
ALSO MADE SINGLE SIZE 40 IN. WIDE
OTHER DIMENSIONS THE SAME . . $26.00

TRADE-MARK REG'D   IN U.S. PATENT OFFICE

GUSTAV STICKLEY

No. 922
BED $36.00
HEADBOARD 54 IN. HIGH
LENGTH 75 IN. (INSIDE)
WIDTH 54 IN (INSIDE)
SINGLE SIZE $30.00
HEADBOARD 50 IN. HIGH
LENGTH 75 IN. (INSIDE)
WIDTH 40 IN. (INSIDE)

922

907

905

No. 907
DRESSING TABLE $38.00
TOP OF MIRROR 54 IN. HIGH
TABLE 30 IN. HIGH, 48 IN. WIDE, 22 IN. DEEP
GLASS 38 IN. X 20 IN.

No. 905
DRESSER $65.00
TOP OF MIRROR 62 IN. HIGH
TABLE 33 IN. HIGH, 48 IN. WIDE, 22 IN. DEEP
GLASS 34 IN. X 26 IN.

TRADE- IN U.S.
MARK PATENT
REG'D OFFICE

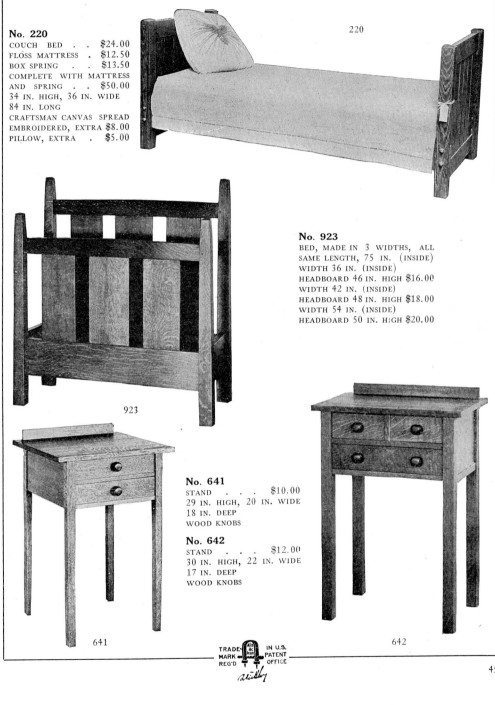

No. 220

COUCH BED	. .	$24.00
FLOSS MATTRESS	.	$12.50
BOX SPRING	. .	$13.50

COMPLETE WITH MATTRESS
AND SPRING . . $50.00
34 IN. HIGH, 36 IN. WIDE
84 IN. LONG
CRAFTSMAN CANVAS SPREAD
EMBROIDERED, EXTRA $8.00
PILLOW, EXTRA . $5.00

220

No. 923

BED, MADE IN 3 WIDTHS, ALL
SAME LENGTH, 75 IN. (INSIDE)
WIDTH 36 IN. (INSIDE)
HEADBOARD 46 IN. HIGH $16.00
WIDTH 42 IN. (INSIDE)
HEADBOARD 48 IN. HIGH $18.00
WIDTH 54 IN. (INSIDE)
HEADBOARD 50 IN. HIGH $20.00

923

No. 641

STAND . . . $10.00
29 IN. HIGH, 20 IN. WIDE
18 IN. DEEP
WOOD KNOBS

No. 642

STAND . . . $12.00
30 IN. HIGH, 22 IN. WIDE
17 IN. DEEP
WOOD KNOBS

641

642

GUSTAV STICKLEY

No. 906
CHEST OF DRAWERS $48.00
46 IN. HIGH, 41 IN. WIDE, 21 IN. DEEP

No. 913
CHEST OF DRAWERS $39.00
51 IN. HIGH, 36 IN. WIDE, 20 IN. DEEP
WOOD KNOBS

906

908

909

913

No. 909
CHEST OF DRAWERS $26.00
42 IN. HIGH, 36 IN. WIDE, 20 IN. DEEP

No. 908
STANDARD MIRROR $7.00
22 IN HIGH, 23 IN. WIDE
GLASS 18 IN. X 14 IN.

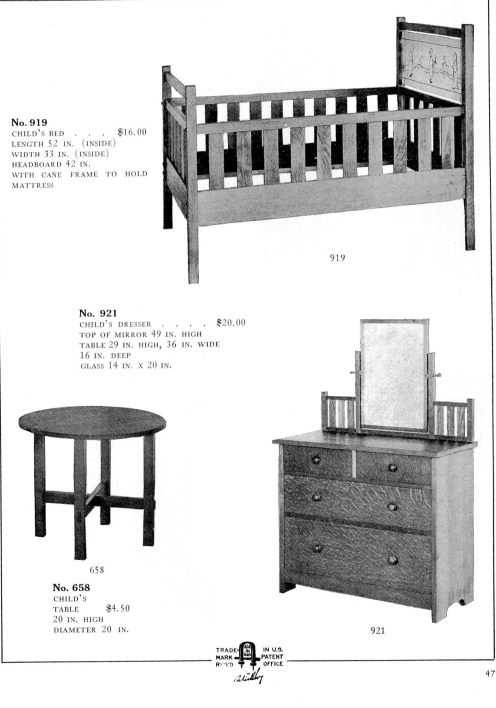

No. 919

CHILD'S BED . . . $16.00
LENGTH 52 IN. (INSIDE)
WIDTH 33 IN. (INSIDE)
HEADBOARD 42 IN.
WITH CANE FRAME TO HOLD
MATTRESS

919

No. 921

CHILD'S DRESSER $20.00
TOP OF MIRROR 49 IN. HIGH
TABLE 29 IN. HIGH, 36 IN. WIDE
16 IN. DEEP
GLASS 14 IN. X 20 IN.

658

No. 658

CHILD'S
TABLE $4.50
20 IN. HIGH
DIAMETER 20 IN.

921

TRADE-
MARK
REG'D

IN U.S.
PATENT
OFFICE

47

GUSTAV STICKLEY

No. 920
CHILD'S WARDROBE . . $36.00
60 IN. HIGH, 34 IN. WIDE,
17 IN. DEEP

920
(OPEN)

No. 388
CHILD'S HIGH
CHAIR . . $9.00
BACK 42 IN. HIGH
SEAT 24 IN. HIGH
15 IN. WIDE
12 IN. DEEP
ADJUSTABLE TRAY
RUSH SEAT

388

920 (CLOSED)

TRADE-
MARK
REG'D

IN U.S.
PATENT
OFFICE

No. 344
CHILD'S ARM CHAIR $4.50
BACK 26 IN. HIGH
SEAT 11 IN. HIGH, 15 IN. WIDE, 12 IN. DEEP

No. 343
CHILD'S ARM ROCKER $4.50
BACK 25 IN. HIGH
SEAT 11 IN. HIGH, 15 IN. WIDE, 12 IN. DEEP
THESE CHAIRS HAVE LEATHER SEATS

344

343

No. 211
CHILD'S SETTLE $8.00
BACK 31 IN. HIGH
SEAT 13 IN. HIGH, 42
IN. WIDE, 12 IN. DEEP

No. 628
CHILD'S TABLE . $8.00
22½ IN. HIGH
36 IN. LONG
22 IN. WIDE

211

628

No. 341
CHILD'S ROCKER . . $3.25
SHEEPSKIN SEAT
BACK 23 IN. HIGH
SEAT 11 IN. HIGH, 13 IN. WIDE,
12 IN. DEEP

No. 640
CHILD'S TABLE . . . $5.00
18 IN. HIGH
28 IN. LONG
20 IN. WIDE

No. 342
CHILD'S CHAIR . . . $3.25
SHEEPSKIN SEAT
BACK 24 IN. HIGH
SEAT 11 IN. HIGH, 13 IN. WIDE.
12 IN. DEEP

341

640

342

TRADE-MARK REG'D IN U.S. PATENT OFFICE

THE CRAFTSMAN FIREPLACE: A COMPLETE HEATING AND VENTILATING SYSTEM

CRAFTSMAN FIREPLACE OF TAPESTRY BRICK, WITH OPEN HEARTH AND ANDIRONS FOR BURNING WOOD

THE Craftsman Fireplace embodies a complete system of both heating and ventilating, combining the efficiency of a furnace with the comfort of an open fire.

Unlike the ordinary furnace, the Craftsman Fireplace can be installed in a main room of the house, thus obviating the need of a cellar and consequent waste of heat, only an ash pit being needed, from which the ashes can be removed each season. The fireplace can be adapted to the burning of wood, coal or coke, by the simple insertion or removal of grates.

The smoke and air openings being properly proportioned, there is no danger of the fireplace smoking. Each smoke compartment is self-closing, back drafts cannot force smoke, dust or ashes into the rooms, and sparks cannot escape through the flue, removing all possibility of fire on the roof.

One fireplace will heat a six or seven-room house, with a consumption of from seven to ten tons of coal per year in a climate like that of our Central States. The exact amount of fuel depends largely upon the exposure, number and size of the windows, and the construction of the house.

The heater can be installed by any mason,

150

No. 150

FIRE SET COMPLETE, . . $22.00
SHOVEL . . 3.50
POKER, . . 2.50
TONGS, . . 4.00
BRUSH, . . 4.00
STAND, . . 8.00
ALL IN WROUGHT IRON
EACH 34 IN. HIGH.
STAND AT BASE, 15½ x 10 IN.

No. 100

ANDIRONS $30.00
WROUGHT IRON, 16 IN. HIGH, 23 IN. DEEP, BASE 5½ x 3½ IN.

either in a house already built or in a new one. With the exception of certain inside measurements, there are no limitations as to the design of the chimneypiece, the cost varying according to the materials chosen. Where there is a cellar and the chimney is carried up two stories, the cost, for brickwork, including brick, sand, cement, flue lining and labor, would be about $65.00.

The price of the steel heater complete with grates, registers and all metal parts (except the pipes needed to conduct warm air from the heater to rooms distant from it) amounts with freight, to $180.00. By combining this with the cost of the brickwork and the pipes, the heating plant complete can be easily installed for about $250.00.

The fireplace is sold only direct to users. I require the plans of each house in which it is to be installed, and from them I make and furnish free to the owner a heating layout which shows the location and size of warm air pipes and registers, and includes complete plans and instructions for the mason to use in building the chimney. I guarantee the fireplace to heat and ventilate properly each house in which it is installed, and by making the heating plant myself and selling it direct to users, I am in a position to assume the entire responsibility of its giving satisfaction.

I shall be glad to hear from all who are considering the installation of heating and ventilating systems.

TRADE-MARK REG'D   IN U.S. PATENT OFFICE

51

EXAMPLES OF CHARACTERISTIC CRAFTSMAN HOMES

BRICK BUNGALOW WITH CYPRESS GABLES, NO. 129, PUBLISHED IN THE CRAFTSMAN, FEBRUARY, 1912.

A TYPICAL CRAFTSMAN BUNGALOW OF BRICK WITH MANY BUILT-IN FITTINGS

A FRESH point of view toward life is what Gustav Stickley presents in the Craftsman homes, THE CRAFTSMAN Magazine and Craftsman furniture. He has always believed that a simpler, more natural way of living would be a good thing for the present generation of people. He is opposed to the old theory that complexity leads to happiness and ornamentation to beauty, and his houses, his magazine and his furniture are *all* opposed to it. He believes that in America we should have houses and furnishings suited to our way of living. We are a busy and intelligent people, hence we want comfort, convenience and beauty in our lives. And Mr. Stickley contends that the relation between environment and character is so close that no one can afford to ignore the kind of home he lives in. Hence in the houses he designs he seeks to bring together appropriateness of design, durability of construction, harmony of outline, with the most simple and practical arrangements of floor space, and he seeks to do this through methods of economy and good craftsmanship.

Already he has presented through the medium of THE CRAFTSMAN Magazine 134 of his houses, and each month two additional ones are shown. Mr. Stickley's purpose in the building of these houses is to make them permanent by using the best materials; to make them simple by doing away with all useless partitions and elaborate fittings; to make them beautiful by avoiding meaningless ornamentation and by so employing the materials, themselves, that their inherent beauty combined

LIVING ROOM WITH GLIMPSE OF DINING ROOM AND FIREPLACE NOOK IN BUNGALOW NO. 129: THE USE OF
BRICK IN INTERIOR FINISH IS OF ESPECIAL INTEREST AS A MEDIUM OF STRUCTURAL DECORATION.

with their skilful use will produce decorative results. He believes that through a sincere purpose in construction, a developed understanding of what beauty means, a clear appreciation of real economy, the Craftsman house has been, and will continue to be, a means of satisfying one of the greatest needs of the times—an American home suited to the American people.

Craftsman house No. 129, shown on these pages, is a typical brick bungalow, published in THE CRAFTSMAN for February, 1912. Both interior and exterior show an interesting use of rough-surfaced brick in tones of red and brown, giving a rich sense of warm friendly color; while the built-in furnishings and beam and panel treatment of the interior serve as a link between the structural features and other furniture and fittings. As to the floor plans, a study of them will show a natural, convenient arrangement with no waste space,—features which distinguish all Craftsman houses.

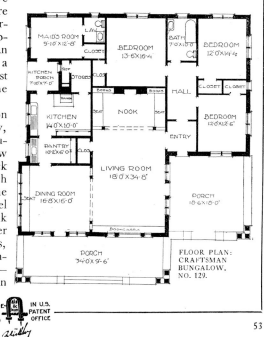

CRAFTSMAN CONCRETE BUNGALOW, NO. 131: AN ECONOMICAL FORM OF CONCRETE CONSTRUCTION IS USED HERE: PUBLISHED IN THE CRAFTSMAN, MARCH, 1912, WITH DESCRIPTION AND DIAGRAMS OF THE PROCESS.

A COMFORTABLE HOMELIKE CONCRETE BUNGALOW

THE bungalow shown here, No. 131, is of cement, built with our new method of concrete construction---a method which is typical of the economy and practical advantage which comes from direct thinking, the touchstone of Craftsman ideas. A complete and continuous insulation is secured here between the two concrete faces of the exterior walls, which are cast in removable and interchangeable forms and left smooth and completely reinforced.

The floor space has been planned with a view to the maximum comfort and convenience of the household. The ample porches, each so effectively sheltered by its recessed walls that it forms practically an outdoor living room, the pleasant and somewhat unique arrangement of the roomy fireplace nook—these are characteristic features of a Craftsman interior.

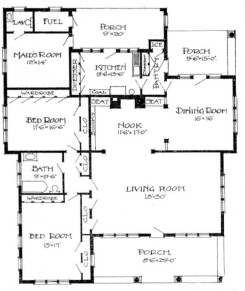

FLOOR PLAN OF CRAFTSMAN CONCRETE BUNGALOW, NO. 131.

THE small bungalow illustrated here, (No. 80), is built of cement and is especially suitable for rural surroundings. The broad porch is sheltered by the extending roof, and inside is a hospitable open fireplace. The arrangement of the floor plan is very simple, comprising a large living room, kitchen, two bedrooms, bath and closets. This little dwelling is especially attractive on account of the combination of comfort, convenience and low cost of construction, which is estimated at from $900 to $1500.

CEMENT BUNGALOW, NO. 80, PUBLISHED IN THE CRAFTSMAN, DECEMBER, 1909. AN ECONOMICAL, COMFORTABLE FOUR-ROOM DWELLING.

SHINGLE COTTAGE, NO. 78, PUBLISHED IN THE CRAFTSMAN, NOVEMBER, 1909.

HOUSE No. 78 is a comfortable, roomy cottage of shingle construction, distinctively Craftsman in its design. The long broad porch, sheltered by the overhang of the main roof, affords ample opportunity for outdoor living, and the dormers above give head room to the bedrooms on the second story.

Economy of space and compactness of arrangement characterize the floor plans, the hall on the first floor serving as a connecting link between dining room and living room and accentuating the sense of spaciousness. Both these rooms, as well as one of the bedrooms upstairs, have open fireplaces, and the wall spaces are filled with practical built-in furnishings,—sideboard and china closets in the dining room, and window seat and bookcases in the living room; all of which will reduce the expense of furnishing, besides adding to the general comfort and beauty of the interior.

FLOOR PLANS OF CRAFTSMAN SHINGLE COTTAGE, NO. 78.

The kitchen is provided with convenient equipment for housework, and a roomy pantry communicates with kitchen and dining room.

TRADE-MARK REG'D IN U.S. PATENT OFFICE

THE CRAFTSMAN PROPOSITION: CRAFTSMAN HOUSE PLANS AND HOW TO SECURE THEM

IN all creative activities with which he is identified, Gustav Stickley is working for the progress of the people. His magazine, THE CRAFTSMAN, is published in the interest of a better, simpler and more reasonable way of living; his houses are designed to bring about this end; his furniture is made in harmony with this ideal. His purpose to establish genuine home conditions has become a religion with him. Naturally, with this ideal in view, he desires to widen the range of his influence. He wants his work in the direction of a finer democracy of home life to count. He wants to reach just as many people who are interested in this sort of life as possible.

In order to put into the hands of every individual interested, actual plans of the kind of home he advocates, he is giving all subscribers to his magazine the floor plans complete of any one of the 134 Craftsman houses which have been shown in the magazine, or of any one of those which will appear in the future numbers, (two new houses being published each month).

Mr. Stickley believes that those of his subscribers who want the sort of homes he is designing will find the use of these plans most advantageous, as he not only furnishes the set complete, but is willing to coöperate heartily in the way of suggestion and advice with architect, contractor or builder.

The plans which he sends are complete working drawings, showing the details of construction and embodying a most economical arrangement of floor space. Hundreds of these house plans have been furnished to subscribers, and have always given satisfaction. The advantage of the present offer will be obvious when it is remembered that each set of plans would probably cost from $50 up if ordered separately.

Each plan embodies typical features of Craftsman architecture; the presence of one or more open fireplaces around which centers the interest of the home; an inglenook, or built-in seats and bookshelves, which carry out the structural design of the rooms and give opportunities for an interesting and decorative use of the woodwork of the interior; the absence of all unnecessary partitions, especially in the main living rooms, resulting in a sense of spaciousness and hospitality; ample opportunity for privacy and quiet in other parts of the house; the simplifying of communication between the different rooms; the utilization of all the available floor space in the most practical and convenient manner, and the provision of as much porch room as possible, so that there may be airy and yet sheltered places for outdoor life, for dining, working, playing and sleeping in the open air. In every instance the effort has been so to arrange the various rooms with relation to each other, and so to plan whatever built-in fittings they may contain, that the work of housekeeping will be rendered as light as possible. In some cases the cottages and bungalows are intended especially for small families where no maid is kept. The equipment of the service portion of the house is always given careful consideration, and a kitchen porch is provided wherever possible, so that many household tasks may be done out of doors. There are plenty of closets and other storage places, and usually a pantry, the kitchen being arranged so that cooking odors can be shut off from the rest of the house.

TO SECURE THE HOUSE PLANS YOU MAY EITHER
(1) SUBSCRIBE TO THE CRAFTSMAN MAGAZINE AT $3.00, OR
(2) ACCEPT OUR COMBINATION OFFER OF THE CRAFTSMAN MAGAZINE AND MR. STICKLEY'S NEW BOOK, "MORE CRAFTSMAN HOMES," AT $3.75.

THE PURPOSE OF THE CRAFTSMAN MAGAZINE

THE CRAFTSMAN magazine is founded on the same principles that rule the designing and making of Craftsman furniture, and it is published for the purpose of giving the broadest and most comprehensive expression to the Craftsman idea. As the principles of honesty, simplicity and directness underlie all that count in thought, life and work, the scope of the magazine includes anything which seems to be an honest expression of direct thought or endeavor. The magazine was first published in October, 1901, as an exponent of the ideals of craftsmanship in this country. It has grown steadily, until today it is recognized as the creator of a movement in America toward the development of a style of architecture which shall be the true expression of the character and needs of the American people.

In addition to this devotion to the demo-

"MADONNA OF THE LAUREL" LOUIS D. VAILLANT, PAINTER: FRONTISPIECE OF THE CRAFTSMAN FOR MAY, 1912.

THE ENTRANCE TO A SIMPLE HOUSE IN AN OLD-FASHIONED GARDEN: FRONTISPIECE OF THE CRAFTSMAN FOR APRIL, 1912.

cratic spirit in architecture, THE CRAFTSMAN Magazine is an ardent advocate of a national art for this country. It has worked from the beginning for better housing and better planning of cities and towns. It advocates the restoration of small farming according to modern improved methods. It seeks steadily to increase the interest in rural living; it gives practical encouragement to the revival of handicrafts, and practical craft workers will find in it information and suggestions of real importance. Among the other valuable features are articles about planting, gardening, protection of birds and conservation of national resources. Its fiction and poetry are modern, realistic, always with the underlying humanitarian purpose.

Among those who have contributed articles on important themes,—social, educational, architectural,—are such recognized

TRADE-MARK REG'D IN U.S. PATENT OFFICE

GUSTAV STICKLEY

earnest thinkers and workers as Jacob A. Riis, William Allen White, Robert Henri, Gutzon Borglum, William L. Price, Walter A. Dyer and Barry Parker.

The three small reproductions given here, which have been selected from recent issues of THE CRAFTSMAN, give a general though inadequate idea of the variety and quality of the illustrations published in the magazine. Each number contains in addition to numerous line drawings, many such half-tones, printed on a rich coated paper in brown duo-tone ink, always embodying the highest quality of workmanship which engraver, printer and editor can achieve, and covering a wide range of subjects.

A gain of 51 per cent. in subscriptions during January, 1912, as compared with January, 1911, a further gain of 101 per cent. in February, 1912, over February of last year, and still greater progress this March, shows, we think, a remarkable popular endorsement of our work, and lends weight to an opinion expressed some time ago by the most impartial body of magazine experts in the world, the "Union de la Presse Périodique Belge," which summed up one of its official reports as follows:

"After careful comparison of the most important magazines of all countries, we have decided to give the palm to THE CRAFTSMAN, an American publication of which the elegance, dignity and beauty have impressed us ever since our first opportunity of seeing it."

A Western subscriber writes concerning THE CRAFTSMAN:

"I do not feel that I can content myself without a word of appreciation as to the work you are doing. So long as the character of your magazine continues to manifest its present strength, permanency and educational value, that long you may consider me an enthusiastic adherent and a regular subscriber. It is a rare thing in this slipshod age to find the doctrine of thoroughness so consistently advocated; and when to the qualities above mentioned is added that of artistic merit, the result is an invaluable paper."

A Canadian subscriber, in renewing his subscription for three years, says:

"I certainly must congratulate you on the excellent magazine. The February number, which contains several very interesting articles especially dealing with English and German modern villages, is particularly pleasing and has been very much appreciated by the members of the Civic Committee on a similar project connected with this city."

A new subscriber, having received a specimen CRAFTSMAN, in sending his subscription, writes:

"THE CRAFTSMAN is certainly one of the finest magazines I have seen, and I read a good many of them, American, German and French."

We should be glad to bear out this endorsement by supplying a copy of THE CRAFTSMAN to those who are interested. The yearly subscription is $3.00.

GUSTAV STICKLEY   THE CRAFTSMAN
41 West 34th Street,   New York City

NEST OF THE GROUND WARBLER: AN ILLUSTRATION IN THE CRAFTSMAN FOR MAY, 1912.

TRADE-MARK REG'D   IN U.S. PATENT OFFICE

OUR NEW BOOK: "MORE CRAFTSMAN HOMES"

"MORE CRAFTSMAN HOMES" is intended to help people who want to build real houses to live in; houses that are durable, beautiful, comparatively inexpensive and always convenient; a type of house that is so suited to family life and so lends itself to the needs and comforts of its inmates, that it may be said to belong to a national style of home architecture, having as its basis a frank and full recognition of the natural and ordinary family needs.

CRAFTSMAN CEMENT HOUSE, NO. 79, PUBLISHED IN THE CRAFTSMAN, NOVEMBER, 1909.

In this book seventy-eight houses are shown, with over four hundred illustrations, including drawings of exteriors and interiors, details of entrances, floor plans and many photographic suggestions for fittings and furnishings.

There are dwellings for town and country, for narrow city lots, suburban, village and rural sites. The materials used include cement, stone, brick, clapboard, shingle and log, alone and in various combinations. The character, size and cost of the designs are varied enough to reach the taste, needs and incomes of practically all home-seekers who are looking for plans which will embody comfort, simplicity and structural quality. Two and three-story houses are shown, suitable for various localities; there are large, roomy buildings for families of ample means, and small, compact cottages for those of more moderate income. Bungalows of different sizes and materials are given, both for permanent occupancy and for week-end and summer use, including a number of delightful suggestions for log homes and woodland camps. Many farmhouses are included, as well as two country schools, one of shingle and the other of logs. "More Craftsman Homes" is printed on a rich coated paper, with cover in craft tones, 201 pages and a portrait of Gustav Stickley. The book, which is $8\frac{1}{2}$ x 11 inches, is put together durably and beautifully, and is intended for library use as well as for the builder's table. Price $2.00 net. Postage prepaid.

FIREPLACE NOOK IN CEMENT HOUSE NO. 79: A CHARACTERISTIC CRAFTSMAN INTERIOR.

TRADE MARK REG'D   IN U.S. PATENT OFFICE

HOW CRAFTSMAN FURNITURE IS FINISHED

THE friendliness and quality of Craftsman furniture depend much upon the finish that is given the wood of which it is made. Here art must come to the aid of nature and help us to produce a finish that will give to the oak the mellow appearance of age without in any way altering the character of the wood. At the same time this finish must protect the wood from soil and moisture.

It was discovered by accident some years ago in England that new oak exposed to the fumes of ammonia would take on a beautiful mellow brown tone. Therefore, as soon as a piece of Craftsman furniture is made, it is first moistened all over to open the pores, and then put into an air-tight compartment, inside which are liberated the fumes of very strong (26 per cent.) ammonia. The time usually demanded for this fuming is forty-eight hours, but that is varied according to the wood and the depth of color required. After the fuming, the wood is carefully sand-papered by hand until the loose fiber is rubbed away and every trace of roughness is removed.

The color, however, given to the wood by this fuming process, is of an uneven tone, and moreover, it is not entirely permanent, in time being gradually absorbed by the wood so that the surface becomes somewhat lighter. Additional color must be added, therefore, which will give a permanent and more uniform tone.

For years I worked and experimented to find the right kind of finish and I have at last succeeded. Craftsman Lustre, the result of my experiments, has just the necessary qualities, for it preserves and emphasizes the natural beauty and sheen of the wood while protecting it from damp and stain.

In applying Craftsman Lustre, when a brown stain is desired, a little asphaltum varnish is added to the Lustre, and when a darker or seal brown is wanted, a small quantity of ultramarine blue is added with the asphaltum varnish. By combining these two tints in different proportions various shades of brown can be obtained. If a green stain is needed, the right amount of green coloring is mixed with the Lustre, which is thus a combined stain and polish.

Furniture-makers who are called upon to supply small pieces to match Craftsman furniture, and others who wish to repolish furniture or to apply a Craftsman stain to interior woodwork, frequently ask me to supply them with the necessary finish. For this reason I am now putting Craftsman Lustre upon the market. It can be supplied either in the clear state or with the required color added, and can be shipped in any quantities upon receipt of orders.

The Lustre is the best floor polish we know of, and can be used in restoring, repairing and repolishing all kinds of furniture and woodwork. Those who are already familiar with the appearance and lasting qualities of the finish of Craftsman furniture will need no further assurance of its efficiency. Samples will be sent upon application.

THIS IS THE LABEL UNDER WHICH CRAFTSMAN LUSTRE IS SOLD.

A FEW CRAFTSMAN LANTERNS AND TABLE LAMPS

777

509

THESE ARE MERELY A FEW EXAMPLES OF OUR METAL WORK. WE ARE PLANNING TO BRING OUT A LARGE LINE OF ELECTRIC TABLE LAMPS AND LAMP SHADES, VARYING FROM 10 TO 22 IN. IN DIAMETER. THE SHADES WILL BE SOLD WITH OR WITHOUT LAMPS

No. 502

ELECTRIC LAMP, GLASS SHADE $15.00 HEIGHT 17 IN., BASE 7 IN. X 7 IN. DIAMETER OF SHADE 12 IN. STAND OF WOOD BANDED WITH COPPER AT THE TOP AND BOTTOM OF THE SHAFT. SHADE OF SMALL PANES OF OPALESCENT GLASS SET IN COPPER

No. 777

ELECTRIC LANTERN, COMPLETE WITH CANOPY AND CHAIN OF SAME METAL AS LANTERN, IN COPPER OR BRASS . $25.00 HEIGHT OF LANTERN 14 IN., BASE 7 IN. SQUARE, MOSAIC FAVRILE GLASS PANELS

502

No. 509

ELECTRIC LANTERN WITH BRACKET COPPER OR BRASS . . . $8.00 IRON . . . . $7.00 HEIGHT OF BRACKET 10 IN., PROJECTION OF BRACKET 7 IN., HEIGHT OF LANTERN 7 IN., BASE $4\frac{1}{2}$ IN. SQR. PANELS OF AMBER TINTED HAMMERED GLASS $4\frac{1}{2}$ IN. SQUARE, BOUND IN METAL, SWINGING LOOSE FROM RIM

50

294

No. 294

OIL LAMP WITH BASE AND FOUNT OF HAMMERED COPPER, HANDLES AND DECORATION IN WROUGHT IRON. SHADE NO. 669, OF JAPANESE WICKER. HEIGHT OF LAMP TO TOP OF BURNER 16 IN. PRICE OF LAMP COMPLETE WITH SHADE . $20.00 PRICE OF SHADE $4.00

No. 50

ELECTRIC LAMP COPPER . . $18.50 21 IN. HIGH OVER ALL DIAMETER AT BASE 7 IN. 3 LIGHTS AND PULL CHAIN

TRADE- IN U.S. MARK PATENT REG'D OFFICE

SIX PIECES OF CRAFTSMAN WILLOW FURNITURE

60

THE right kind of willow furniture affords exactly the relief that is necessary to lighten the general effect of the darker and heavier oak pieces of Craftsman furniture. In fact, we have come to believe that a room, to be satisfactorily furnished, should have one or two pieces of willow among the oak. Especially is it desirable in combination with our heavier style, for it adds a note of decorative charm and a touch of lighter color to the more solid and dignified furniture of wood. At the same time it is as simple in line and as natural in finish as the more severe and massive oaken chairs and settles.

Our willow pieces, some of which are shown here, while strongly and firmly made, have yet the flexibility of a well-woven basket. They are finished in two colors, a soft green and a deep golden brown. In both cases the color is more or less uneven,

No. 82
WILLOW CHAIR $18.00
BACK 41 IN. HIGH
SEAT 17 IN. HIGH, 20 IN. WIDE, 18 IN. DEEP

No. 83
WILLOW ROCKER $18.00 (SAME DESIGN AND DIMENSIONS AS NO. 82)

No. 60
WILLOW CHAIR $24.50
BACK 39 IN. HIGH. ARMS 30 IN. HIGH
SEAT 17 IN. HIGH, 22 IN. WIDE, 23 IN. DEEP

No. 54½
WILLOW CHAIR $14.00
BACK 33 IN. HIGH
SEAT 17 IN. HIGH, 20 IN. WIDE, 19 IN. DEEP

82

54½

TRADE-MARK REG'D IN U.S. PATENT OFFICE

varying as it might in the branches themselves.

The cushions are covered with Craftsman canvas, but of course these coverings either in color or material could be varied to suit any scheme of furnishing. For a summer cottage or bungalow a chintz or cretonne is particularly attractive for the cushion coverings. The prices quoted include cushions.

While Craftsman willow furniture forms a welcome addition to any interior, it is equally suitable for the summer home, the seaside cottage or country bungalow. For veranda, balcony and open-air living room it would be difficult to find anything more comfortable and appropriate, particularly in States where the warm sunny climate permits much outdoor life.

64

56

No. 64
WILLOW CHAIR $22.50
BACK 33 IN. HIGH,
ARMS 28 IN. HIGH
SEAT 17 IN. HIGH, 21 IN. WIDE, 23 IN. DEEP

No. 56
WILLOW CHAIR $20.00
ARMS 31 IN. HIGH
SEAT 17 IN. HIGH, 22 IN. WIDE, 23 IN. DEEP.

No. 72
WILLOW SETTLE $43.00
BACK 33 IN. HIGH
ARMS 28 IN. HIGH
SEAT 17 IN. HIGH, 54 IN. LONG,
26 IN. DEEP
LENGTH OVER ALL 66 IN.

TRADE-MARK REG'D IN U.S. PATENT OFFICE

70

No. 70

SETTLE, INCLUDING TWO
PILLOWS . . $68.00
BACK 32 IN. HIGH
SEAT 17 IN. HIGH, 78 IN.
LONG, 27 IN. DEEP
LENGTH OVER ALL 86 IN.

ECONOMICAL UPHOLSTERY OF FABRIKOID LEATHER

MANY people cannot afford to use real leather in the furnishing and decoration of their homes, but would be glad of some equally durable and beautiful material as a less expensive substitute. Fabrikoid Leather was made to fill this need. It is an artificial leather designed especially for upholstery work. It not only costs less than hide leather, but in many cases is more satisfactory, being non-absorbent, water and vermin proof. It will not stretch out of shape, and being of uniform strength and thickness and convenient size it can be cut without waste.

The screen shown here merely illustrates one of the many uses to which Fabrikoid Leather can be put. It can be used for the seats, backs and cushions of chairs and settles, for desk and table tops, wall papering and paneling.

Fabrikoid Leather is suitable for any interior where an effective and economical form of upholstery is desired—in town or country houses, club rooms, etc., and especially in summer bungalows which, being occupied during only a part of the year, must not incur too much expense in the furnishing. The closing of the bungalow for the winter months would not hurt the Fabrikoid Leather, as it is uninjured by neglect, damp, dust or vermin.

No. 83F

SCREEN, PANELED IN FABRIKOID LEATHER . $22.00
66 IN. HIGH, THREE PANELS, EACH 22 IN. WIDE

TRADE-MARK REG'D IN U.S. PATENT OFFICE

The Craftsman

DEPARTMENT OF INTERIOR FURNISHINGS

THE CRAFTSMAN BUILDING
6 EAST 39th STREET, NEW YORK

INSTRUCTIONS TO OUR PATRONS

HOW TO ORDER FROM THIS CATALOGUE

It will facilitate matters in our Order Department if the fullest instructions are given in ordering any piece shown here. We would like not only the piece number and the letter D, but also the page number on which the article is illustrated.

Where any number of articles are shown in one picture, they are numbered from left to right.

Address all orders to:
The Craftsman Department of Interior Furnishings, Craftsman Building, 6 East 39th Street, New York.

CRAFTSMAN WILLOW WORK

THE Craftsman Department of Interior Furnishings shows in this catalogue what it has accomplished since the opening of the new Craftsman Building. The furniture, fabrics, pottery, lamps, baskets, china, silverware and glass illustrated have been assembled by us, and from our point of view, represent some of the finest specimens of interior furniture and fittings manufactured in this country. Many of these examples of fine craftsmanship are from our own workshops; others are designed and produced by various distinguished makers.

We especially wish to call your attention to the convincing artistic merit of these articles which are all "made in America." We feel very proud that our country holds a place second to none in the beauty as well as comfort of its home furnishings and decorations.

Your order will command our most careful attention, and when it is not possible to give immediate delivery you will receive word at once when you may expect shipment. Of course, where certain stocks have been oversold, our patrons will realize that orders must be filled in their turn.

We hope not only that this little booklet will prove of interest, but that through it we may be of real service to you.

THE CRAFTSMAN

DEPARTMENT OF INTERIOR FURNISHINGS

No. **6** D. This Dining Room Suite marks a new and interesting departure in Craftsman Furniture: Broad bands of wood with up-and-down grain add to the beauty of the fumed oak: The suite comprises Table, Sideboard, China Cabinet, five Side Chairs and one Armchair. Price, in Oak.......**$175.00** In Mahogany ....**$210.00** The serving table is extra— In Oak ....**$25.00** In Mahogany **$30.00**

No. **6** D. Serving Table, 38 in. high, 42 in. wide, 18 in. deep: In Oak.........**$25.00** In Mahogany **$30.00**

No. **6** D. Armchair, 37 in. high, seat 20½ in. wide, 18½ in. deep, 18½ in. high: Slip Seat Cushion of Craftsman Leather, Brown or Green: In Oak.................**$12.00** In Mahogany **$14.00**

No. **6** D. Sideboard, with Brass Trim: 43 in. high, 56 in. long, 22 in. deep: In Oak....................**$53.00** In Mahogany **$60.00**

GUSTAV STICKLEY—THE CRAFTSMAN

No. **6** D. Chair, 34 in. high, seat 18 in. wide, 16½ in. deep, 18½ in. high: Slip Seat Cushion of Craftsman Leather, Brown or Green: In Oak..........**$8.00**
In Mahogany **$9.50**

No. **6** D. China Cabinet with Adjustable Shelves: Back lined with Velvet any color desired: 60 in. high, 40 in. wide, 13 in. deep: In Oak..........**$40.00**
In Mahogany **$48.00**

No. **6** D. Dining Table, Oval, particularly suitable for oblong room: 48 in. wide, 62 in. long, extending to 8 ft. The three leaves can be stored under the top, concealed: In Oak **$38.00**
In Mahogany, **$45.00**
The table may also be had circular 48 in. diameter.

5

DEPARTMENT OF INTERIOR FURNISHINGS

No. **7** D. Gumwood Writing Table, 42 in. wide, 23 in. deep, 30 in. high..........**$35.00**

In Mahogany **$42.00**

No. **8** D. Gumwood or Oak Rocker, 34 in. high, seat 16 in. deep, 16½ in. wide, 15 in. high **$8.00**

In Mahogany **$9.50**

No. **9** D. Gumwood Table, 25½ in. high, 24 in. wide, 17 in. deep **$7.00**

In Mahogany **$8.50**

No. **10** D. Gumwood or Oak Desk Chair, 40 in. high, seat 16 in. deep, 16½ in. wide, 18½ in. high..........**$7.50**

In Mahogany **$9.00**

GUSTAV STICKLEY—THE CRAFTSMAN

No. **11** D. Gumwood Writing Table, 29 in. high, 34 in. wide, 21 in. deep **$17.50**
In Mahogany.**$21.00**
(Desk chair described on page 6.)

No. **12** D. Gumwood Bedside Stand, 28½ in. high, top 16 in. square **$7.00**

No. **13** D. Gumwood Side Table, 30 in. high, 28 in. wide, 18 in. deep **$8.50**
In Mahogany.**$10.00**

No. **14** D. Gumwood or Oak Side Chair, 36 in. high, seat 16 in. deep, 16½ in. wide, 18 in. high, **$7.50**
In Mahogany..**$9.00**

These chairs have loose seats, upholstered in color and material to order.

DEPARTMENT OF INTERIOR FURNISHINGS

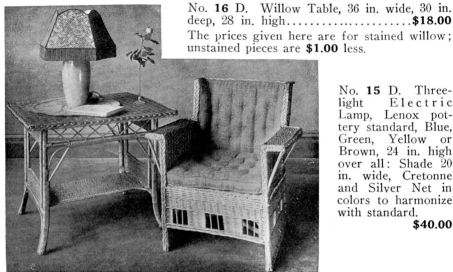

No. **16** D. Willow Table, 36 in. wide, 30 in. deep, 28 in. high....................**$18.00**
The prices given here are for stained willow; unstained pieces are **$1.00** less.

No. **15** D. Three-light Electric Lamp, Lenox pottery standard, Blue, Green, Yellow or Brown, 24 in. high over all: Shade 20 in. wide, Cretonne and Silver Net in colors to harmonize with standard.
$40.00

No. **18** D. Willow Chair (below), 34 in. high, seat 17 in. wide, 17 in. deep, 17 in. high, with Velour cushion, **$8.75**

No. **17** D. Willow Armchair (above), 33 in. high, arms 24 in. high, seat 17 in. high, 21 in. wide, 22 in. deep, upholstered in Velour **$23.00**

No. **19** D. Willow Scrap Basket,
8 in. diameter **$2.00**
12 in. diameter ... **3.00**
14 in. diameter ... **3.50**

No. **20** D. Willow Table, 26 in. diameter, 29 in. high **$8.50**

(This Table is shown below.)

No. **21** D. Willow Armchair, 34 in. high, arms 24 in. high, seat 15 in. high, 21 in. wide, 19 in. deep, Velour cushion, **$15.00**

GUSTAV STICKLEY—THE CRAFTSMAN

No. **22** D. Willow Muffin Stand, 36 in. high **$5.00**

No. **23** D. Willow Three-Light Electric Piano Lamp, 70 in. high over all; shade 24 in: diameter, lined with silk to match stain of willow, **$27.50**

No. **24** D. Willow Armchair, 36 in. high, arms 28½ in. high, seat 14½ in. high, 22½ in. wide, 23½ in. deep, in velour.......**$22.50**

No. **26** D. Velour Pillows, shown in lower picture, each, **$6.00**

No. **27** D. Cretonne Pillows, each **$3.50**

No. **25** D. Willow Day-Bed (shown above), 86 in. long over all, 30 in. deep, ends 29 in. high, seat 18 in. high: pocket and shelf in each end upholstered in Velour **$58.00**

9

DEPARTMENT OF INTERIOR FURNISHINGS

No. **29** D. Willow Sandwich Basket (at left of table), 10 in. diameter.
$1.25

No. **30** D. Willow Flower Basket (center of table), 8 in. diameter **$1.50**

No. **31** D. Willow Flower or Fruit Basket (at right of table), 15 in. long......**$1.85**

No. **28** D. Nest of Oak Tables, largest 29 in. high, 24 in. wide, 17 in. deep, set....**$12.00**
In Mahogany...**$14.00**

No. **34** D. Scrap Basket (at right of picture, on floor), 12 in. diameter ...**$3.00**

No. **32** D. Willow Scrap Basket (at left of picture, on floor), 12 in. diameter,
$2.50

No. **33.** Willow Bread Basket (center of picture on floor), 12 in. long,
$1.35

No. **35** D. Gumwood or Oak Dressing Table, 40 in. wide, 21 in. deep, 28½ in. high: height to top of mirror 56 in.......**$34.00**
In Mahogany......**$40.00**

No. **36** D. Cream China Gold-Band Candlesticks, 6½ in. high, pair...**$4.00**

GUSTAV STICKLEY—THE CRAFTSMAN

No. **37** D. Gumwood Cabinet (below), 55 in. high, 27 in. wide, 17 in. deep **$32.00**

In Mahogany **$38.00**

Both this Gumwood—or Mahogany—Cabinet and the Chiffonier are finished by the same method as is used with our brown fumed oak, with the result that all the color of the wood is revealed and the surface is left a velvet texture: To those who are interested in this finish we will be glad to send on application a small sample of these woods.

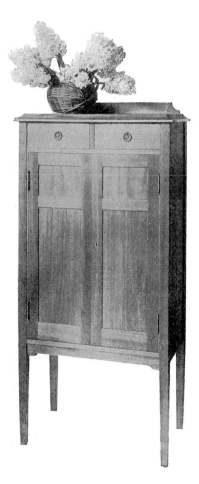

No. **38** D. Gumwood or Oak Chiffonier, 48 in. high, 32 in. wide, 20 in deep..**$30.00**

In Mahogany **$36.00**

The various hues of the gumwood are so well brought out by our method of finishing the wood that it combines interestingly with many different color schemes: In addition to the delicate wood brown there is a suggestion of violet, pale green and blue in the surface so that gumwood furniture is most satisfactory in bedrooms and boudoirs where a finely harmonious color scheme is necessary: The furniture itself is made on fine lines so that both color and construction render it appropriate for elegant furnishing.

11

DEPARTMENT OF INTERIOR FURNISHINGS

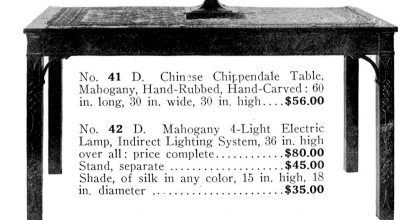

No. **39** D. Chinese Chippendale Armchair, Nut-Brown Mahogany, Hand-Rubbed, Hand-Carved: 39 in. high, seat 27 in. wide, 24 in. deep, 16 in. high: in muslin, **$43.75**

No. **40** D. Chinese Chippendale Armchair, Nut-Brown Mahogany, Hand-Rubbed, Hand-Carved; 36 in. high, seat 27½ in. wide, 24 in. deep, 17 in. high: in muslin, **$40.00**

No. **41** D. Chinese Chippendale Table, Mahogany, Hand-Rubbed, Hand-Carved: 60 in. long, 30 in. wide, 30 in. high....**$56.00**

No. **42** D. Mahogany 4-Light Electric Lamp, Indirect Lighting System, 36 in. high over all: price complete...........**$80.00**
Stand, separate **$45.00**
Shade, of silk in any color, 15 in. high, 18 in. diameter **$35.00**

GUSTAV STICKLEY—THE CRAFTSMAN

No. **44** D. Chinese Chippendale Settee, Nut - Brown Mahogany, Hand - Carved: 76 in. long, 37 in. high, seat 35 in. deep, 17 in. high: in muslin **$84.00**

No. **45** D. Stand, 26 in. wide, 15 in. deep, 27 in. high ...**$28.00**

No. **43** D. Mirror, 38 in. square. **$38.50**

No. **46** D. Chair, 42 in. high, seat 22 in. wide, 18 in. deep, 18 in. high: muslin, **$29.75**

No. **47** D. Arm chair, 43½ in. high, seat 25 in. wide, 18 in. deep, 18 in. high: muslin ..**$37.70**

DEPARTMENT OF INTERIOR FURNISHINGS

No. **61** D. Dark Oak Stand, 29 in. high, top 14 by 15 in., with pocket beneath..**$11.00** (This stand is especially useful for the telephone.)

No. **62** D. Dark Oak Bench, Cane seat, 36 in. long, 14 in. deep, 15½ in. high...**$14.00**

No. **63** D. Dark Oak Rocker, Cane seat, sides and back: 35 in. high, seat 21 in. deep, 24½ in. wide, 15 in. high, **$34.00**

No. **64** D. Dark Oak Table, 41 in. long, 29 in. wide, 30 in. high, **$23.00**

This Furniture, of Jacobean inspiration, is attractive for summer with the cane showing. It is richer and warmer for winter with loose cushions, in materials and colors to correspond with the decorations of a room.

No. **65** D. Dark Oak Settle, Cane seat, sides and back: 37 in. high, seat 46 in. long, 22 in. deep, 16 in. high **$60.00**

GUSTAV STICKLEY—THE CRAFTSMAN

No. **67** D. Mahogany
Sewing Table, 30 in. high,
leaves extended 35 in.
$25.00

No. **68** D. Book Ends,
Green Bronze **$5.00**

No. **69** D. Book Ends,
Hand-Painted Flowers,
$5.00

No. **70** D. Book Ends,
Green Bronze (Elephants)
$5.00

No. **71** D. Mahogany
Rocker, 31 in. high, seat
15 in. high and 18 in.
wide **$9.25**

No. **72** D. Mahogany
Chair, 30 in. high, seat 16
in. high and 14 in. wide,
$9.25

No. **73** D. Mahogany
Rocker, 31 in. high, seat
16 in. high and 17 in.
wide **$11.50**

Straight chairs to match rockers, and rocker to match straight chair, same price.

DEPARTMENT OF INTERIOR FURNISHINGS

No. **101** D. One-light Electric Lamp with Fulper Pottery Standard in Dull Green. Willow Shade stained Red or Green, lined with Silk in any desired colors. Diameter of Shade 10½ in.; height over all 15½ in. **$5.00**

(These are only a few examples of our many Lamp designs.)

No. **102** D. Two-light Electric Lamp with Reed Standard, Copper Trim, and Reed Shade stained Brown, Green or Gray; Shade lined with Figured Silk in appropriate tones. Especially suitable for Living Room or Library. Diameter of Shade 20 in.; height over all 19 in. **$15.00**

No. **103** D. One-light Electric Lamp with Fumed Oak Standard, Copper Trim and Willow Shade stained Red or Green, lined with Silk in any colors preferred. Diameter of Shade 10½ in.; height over all 15½ in. **$3.50**

No. **104** D. One-light Electric Lamp with Fumed Oak Standard, Brass Trim and Silk Shade in any colors desired. Diameter of Shade 12 in.; height over all 20 in.; complete **$8.75**; without Shade **$4.00**.

(This lamp is shown at the left.)

No. **105** D. One-light Electric Lamp with Lenox Pottery Standard in White, Blue, Mauve, Gray, Soft Green, Rose, Orange or Brown, with Brass Trim. Shade of Figured Silk in various colors, under Silver Net, with Wooden Beads. A charming Lamp for Bedroom or Boudoir. Diameter of Shade 10½ in.; height over all 17½ in.....**$15.00**

(This Lamp is shown above.)

16

GUSTAV STICKLEY—THE CRAFTSMAN

No. **53** D. Silver Tea Set, 5 pieces (Tea Pot, Coffee Pot, Sugar Bowl, Cream Pitcher and Jar), decorated with a chased shield design, and fitted with ebony handles. Set complete with five pieces **$50.00**
Tea Caddy, extra **7.50**

No. **54** D. Two-Handled Jardinière, Cucumber Green, inside Yellow.**$1.50**

No. **55** D. Gourd-Shaped Bottle, Sky Blue **$1.25**

No. **56** D. Book Ends, soft dull Gray, per set **$3.00**

No. **57** D. Turtle Flower Holder, with holes **$1.00**

No. **58** D. Lily Vase, Green, 7½ in. high **$2.00**

No. **59** D. Flower Holder, dull Green, 12½ in. high **$4.00**

No. **60** D. Flower Holder, Green flambé, 9½ in. high...........**$2.50**

The countless designs, sizes and colors of the pottery in our Department of Interior Furnishings afford a wide range of choice.

17

DEPARTMENT OF INTERIOR FURNISHINGS

No. **74** D.   Lenox Individual Breakfast Set, Cream, with Yellow and Brown Bands, set complete with 10 pieces...... ....**$15.00**

No. **75** D. Vase, Brown, Blue, Orange or Green, 6¼ in. high. **$1.50**

No. **76** D. Flower Holder, Brown, Blue, Orange or Green, 10½ in. high, **$6.00**

No. **77** D. Flower Holder, Blue and B l a c k, 11¾ in. high **$6.00**

No. **78** D. Vase, Brown, Blue, Orange or Green, 8¼ in. high, 3¼ in. diameter ...**$2.25**

No. **79** D. Vase, Brown, Blue, Orange or Green, 12 in. high, 4½ in. diameter ...**$5.00**

These vases are described in order from left to right.

GUSTAV STICKLEY—THE CRAFTSMAN

No. **80** D. Two-Handled Jar, opening 5 in. diameter, Soft-Brown or Green Matte **$5.00**

No. **81** D. Candlesticks, Soft Green, 9½ in. high, per pair **$3.50**

No. **82** D. Low Flower Bowl, Yellow with Sky-Blue Lining, 10½ in. diameter **$4.00**

These vases are described in order from left to right.

No. **83** D. Lily Leaf, Green, to hold Flowers.........................**$0.50**

No. **84** D. Nut Bowl, shaded Soft Green, 6¼ in. diameter.............**$1.75**

No. **85** D. Jar, Soft Yellow, 8 in. high...............................**$4.00**

No. **86** D. Silver Service, Best Plate: five pieces, as illustrated......**$50.50**

19

DEPARTMENT OF INTERIOR FURNISHINGS

No. **87** D. Flower Holder, Brown, Blue, Orange or Green, 9½ in. high, **$1.75**

No. **88** D. Flower Holder, Brown, Blue, Orange or Green, 10 in. high, 3 in. diameter **$3.50**

No. **89** D. Lenox Vase, Black and White, 8 in. high, 4 in. diameter.**$4.50**

No. **90** D. Flower Holder, Pink, 5½ in. high **$4.00**

No. **91** D. Flower Holder, Deep Rich Blue, 7 in. high, **$3.50**

No. **92** D. Flower Holder, Brown, Blue, Orange or Green, 10½ in. high, **$2.00**

No. **93** D. Flower Holder, Black and White or Blue and Black, 14½ in. high, 5 in. dia.**$5.00**

No. **94** D. Jardinière, Brown, Blue, Orange or Green, 9½ in. high, 12 in. dia.**$12.00**

No. **95** D. Flower Holder, Brown, Blue, Orange or Green, 15 in. high, 6 in. dia. **$7.00**

No. **96** D. Flower Holder, Brown, Blue, Orange or Green, 12 in. high, 7 in. dia. **$6.00**

No. **97** D. Flower Holder, Brown, Blue, Orange or Green, 8 in. high, 7½ in. dia..**$3.50**

GUSTAV STICKLEY—THE CRAFTSMAN

No. **99** D. Lenox Tea Set, White with Gold Band and Handles, comprising Teapot, Cream Pitcher, Sugar Bowl, 6 Tea Cups and Saucers, 6 After Dinner Cups and Saucers, 6 Plates, and 6 Bread-and-Butter Plates; complete set of 27 pieces ....**$49.00** (Part of this set is shown below.)

No. **100** D. Mahogany, Glass-covered Tray with Brass Handles, 14 in. diameter............**$7.50**

No. **98** D. Lenox Dinner Set (only a few pieces shown), Cream-White, Band of Deeper Cream, with Brown Border; 83 pieces, **$101.00;** other prices upon application; open set. Shown above.

DEPARTMENT OF INTERIOR FURNISHINGS

No. **48** D. Fumed Oak Chair, 38 in. high, seat 16½ in. deep, 17 in. high, 20 in. diameter...**$10.00**

In Mahogany ...**$12.00**

No. **49** D. Mahogany Rocker, 31 in. high, seat 15 in. high, 19 in. diameter **$18.00**

(Straight Chair to Match, same price.)

These pieces give some idea of the wide variety of styles to be found in the Craftsman Department of Interior Furnishings.

No. **50** D. Mahogany Tip Table, 28 in. high, 28 in. diameter......**$17.50**

No. **51** D. Mahogany Chippendale Pedestal, 36 in. high, base 15 in. diameter **$39.00**

No. **52** D. Mahogany Chair, 32 in. high, seat 18 in. high, 18 in. diameter **$15.00**

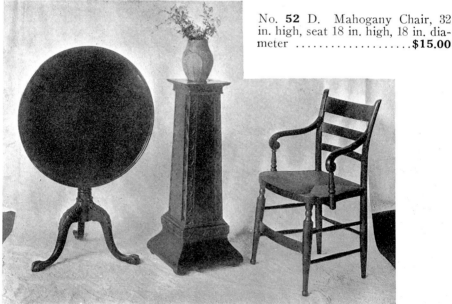

GUSTAV STICKLEY—THE CRAFTSMAN

No. **106** D. Mahogany Adjustable Reclining Chair, an exact reproduction of the original William Morris' chair: back 41 in. high, seat 16 in. high, 23 in. wide and 41 in. deep. This Chair, which is shown at the left, can be ordered upholstered in any material or colors desired. The cushions are stuffed with hair. The price of the chair upholstered in Velour or Tapestry is **$60.00**

No. **107** D. Three-fold Screen with Gumwood Frame and Cretonne Panels with Wicker in the lower part: The Screen is 66 in. high and each Panel is 24 in. wide. Price **$35.00**

No. **108** D. Willow Settle (shown below), stained in any shade and upholstered in any material and color desired: Back 33 in. high, arms 28 in. high, seat 17 in. high, 54 in. long, 28 in. deep: Length over all 66 in.
Upholstered in Craftsman Linen **$43.00**
Upholstered in Velour 50.00
With Willow Unstained, **$1.00** less.

No. **108½** D. Willow Chair, Stained in any shade and upholstered in any material and color desired: Back 36 in. high, seat 18 in. high, 21 in. wide, 21 in. deep, **$17.00**
In Unstained Willow...... **$16.00**

DEPARTMENT OF INTERIOR FURNISHINGS

No. **109** D. Solid Mahogany Gate-leg Table, top 42 by 42 in. when open ...**$35.00**

This Table is a very popular design, for it is large enough when open to serve as a breakfast or luncheon table, and when the adjustable leaves are closed it can be set aside and will take up very little space.

No. **110** D. Solid Mahogany Desk, 40 in. high, 38 in. wide, 19 in. deep ...**$60.00**

This Desk is unusually capacious, with its three drawers and ample writing space. The inside fittings are very complete and convenient.

GUSTAV STICKLEY—THE CRAFTSMAN

No. **111** D. Gumwood or Oak Wardrobe, 65 in. high, 42 in. wide, 19 in. deep..................**$75.00**
In Mahogany **$90.00**

This new Craftsman Wardrobe which is shown here both closed and open is as practical a piece of furniture as it is attractive. The exterior with its soft finish and simple yet decorative paneling adds an interesting note to the room in which it is placed, while the interior is arranged for the utmost convenience of the user. The drawers are of different sizes, and above them is a hat box, below a place for shoes. The other side is provided with rod and hangers, which are not shown, however, in the illustration. One of the doors is lined with a full length mirror which adds considerably to the usefulness of the piece.

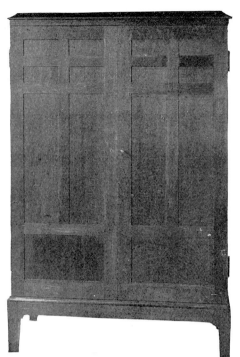

(The illustration below shows wardrobe No. **111** D open.)

DEPARTMENT OF INTERIOR FURNISHINGS

No. **112** D. 8 in. diameter Nappy "Kalana Lily," each **$5.00**

The glassware shown on these pages is all of clear crystal, fine in texture and ornamented with delicate, graceful designs. The illustrations, naturally, give only a faint impression of the charming quality of these pieces.

No. **113** D. Vase, 6 in. high, "Kalana Lily," each **$1.50**
Per dozen **15.00**
(Shown below.)

No. **116½** D. Grapefruit Glass, per dozen **$20.00**. Plate, per dozen **$28.00**.
(These plates are suitable for many uses.)

No. **114** D. Goblet, per dozen, **$14.00**

No. **115** D. Claret or Cocktail Glass, per dozen..**$12.00**

No. **116** D. Finger Bowl, per dozen, **$14.00**
Finger-Bowl Plate, per dozen..**$20.00**

No. **117** D. Water Tumbler, per dozen **$12.00**

GUSTAV STICKLEY—THE CRAFTSMAN

No. **118** D. Mayonnaise Bowl,
each **$2.50**
Plate, each **$2.50**

No. **119** D and No. **120** D. Sugar
Bowl and Cream Pitcher, per set,
$4.00

No. **122** D.
4 in. Vase, each....**$1.00**
5 " " " **1.25**
6 ½" " " **2.00**

The examples of glassware
illustrated in this catalogue
show especially fine and or-
namental work, and indicate
the high degree to which
this craft has been developed in America.

No. **121** D.
5 in. Round Saucer (above),
Per dozen **$20.00**
Each **2.00**

No. **123** D. 6 in.
Comport, each,
$2.50

No. **124** D. In-
dividual Almond,
per dozen,
$9.00

No. **125** D. 4½
in. Sherbert, per
dozen,
$15.00

No. **126** D. Bell
Sherbert,
Per doz., **$12.00**
Plate " 17.00

DEPARTMENT OF INTERIOR FURNISHINGS

No. **127** D. Goblet, per dozen, (shown at the left)......**$12.00**

No. **128** D. 4 in. Sherbert, per dozen, (shown above) **$14.00**
Sherbert Plate, per dozen.........**$16.00**

No. **129** D. Water Tumbler, per dozen, (shown below) **$10.00**

No. **130** D. Goblet, per dozen, (shown at the right)...**$12.00**

No. **131** D.
Finger Bowl, per dozen......**$14.00**
Finger Bowl Plate, per dozen **18.00**
(Shown below.)

No. **132** D.
Tall Ale or
Highball Tumbler, per dozen, (shown at the right) ..**$12.00**

GUSTAV STICKLEY—THE CRAFTSMAN

No. **135** D. Vase (shown below), "Tulip," 8 in., each, **$1.25**. 10 in., each, **$1.50**.

No. **133** D. Vase (shown above), 7 in. high, "Geranium," each **$1.25**

No. **134** D. Vase (shown at the right), 12 in., each...**$3.50**

No. **136** D. Single Flower Vase, Engraved (illustrated at the left).

6 in.	**$1.75**
8 in.	**2.25**
10 in.	**2.50**
15 in.	**3.60**

DEPARTMENT OF INTERIOR FURNISHINGS

No. **137** D. Tea Set, Adams design, Blue and Green, set of 41 pieces, **$150.00**
Open set: Individual prices upon application.

No. **138** D. Yellow Chintz, Flowers and Birds, 31 in. wide, per yd., **$1.00**

No. **139** D. Cotton, Yellow ground with Brown and Pink, 50 in. wide. **$3.00**

No. **140** D. Cretonne, Yellow Daisies, Lavender and Blue, 50 in. wide, per yd......**$2.50**

No. **141** D. Cotton, Silk Stripe, Persian design, Gray, Rose, 46 in. wide, per yd.**$3.50**

GUSTAV STICKLEY—THE CRAFTSMAN

No. **142** D. Lenox Oatmeal Set (Bowl, Saucer, Pitcher, Sugar Bowl) **$2.60**

No. **143** D. Lenox Tea Set (Tea Pot, Sugar Bowl Pitcher, Combined), **$2.25**

No. **144** D. Lenox Loaf Sugar Dish (in the foreground), **$0.90**

No. **145** D. Child's Bread - and - Milk Set (Cup, Bowl, Plate), **$5.00**

No. **146** D. Crossbar Scrim Sundour, 50 in. wide, per yd.............**$0.75**
No. **147** D. Brown Sundour. 36 in. wide, per yd....................**$0.85**
No. **148** D. Sundour Natural, green peacock eyes, 50 in. wide, per yd..**$1.75**
No. **149** D. Natural Linen, green and pink design, 31 in., per yd......**$1.20**

DEPARTMENT OF INTERIOR FURNISHINGS

No. **150** D. Armchair, upholstered in genuine Morocco, stuffed with Silk Floss (shown above)....**$65.00**

Rocker, same style, same price. Settle, same style, 78 in. long...**$170.00**

No. **152** D. English Club Chair, upholstered in genuine Morocco (Stuffed with Down), Blue, Green, Red, or Brown (above).....**$73.00**

No. **151** D. Arm Rocker, upholstered in genuine Morocco, stuffed with Down (shown below)...**$66.00**

Straight Chair, same style, same price. Settle, same style, 58 in. long **$132.00**

No. **153** D. Armchair, upholstered in genuine Morocco, Down Cushion, 31 in. high, 30 in. wide......**$100.00**
(Shown below.)

Settle, same style, 78 in. long,
$198.00

GUSTAV STICKLEY—THE CRAFTSMAN

These chairs are
all of Mahogany.

No. **154** D. Armchair, 40 in. high, 25 in.
wide, seat 17 in. high, 19 in. wide:
In Denim $17.00
In Tapestry or Velour **19.00**

No. **155** D. Rocker, 37 in. high, 25 in.
wide, seat 16 in. high, 19 in. deep:
In Denim $18.50
In Tapestry or Velour **20.00**
　　　　(Both shown above.)

No. **156** D. Rocker, 40 in. high, 25 in.
wide, seat 17 in. high, 19 in. wide:
In Denim $17.00
In Tapestry or Velour **23.00**

No. **157** D. Armchair, 45 in. high, 24 in.
wide, seat 18 in. high, 18 in. deep:
In Denim $27.50
In Tapestry or Velour **34.50**